"The power of this deeply moving and exceptionally well-told story lies in its ability to be a source of healing for anyone who suffers from unhealed hurts. It calls others to experience this truth: pain that is not reflected on and shared will be stripped of its ability to give closure to the past as it opens new doors to life. Fumia leads the reader beyond the darkness of deep inner night to the brightness of hope-filled days."

Paula Ripple, author of
Called to Be Friends and
Growing Strong at Broken Places

"*A Child at Dawn* is a very complex book that I will read again and again and continue to be touched by new images and feelings. Fumia beautifully describes how there are no statutes of limitation on grief and the resolution of pain. Grief just doesn't go away. It spreads out in ever-widening circles connecting our suffering with those who come before us and those who will follow. She shows us that we may find the instruments of healing in unexpected people and places. This is a powerfully moving book which is not only about healing, it is healing."

Martha Manning, Clinical Psychologist,
author of *A Season of Mercy*

"The devastation of the human heart engulfed by grief, loss and separation can render severe emotional blocks to psychospiritual growth. This powerfully written narrative of one mother's search for meaning in the death of her child presents valuable insights for recovery from extended sorrow and inner pain. The message of this book can bring comfort and hope to the grief-stricken, as well as to those who professionally or pastorally care for the dying."

Barbara Leahy Shlemon, author of
Healing Prayer and
Healing the Hidden Self

A Child at Dawn

The Healing of a Memory

Molly Fumia

AVE MARIA PRESS ● Notre Dame, Indiana 46556

About the Author

Married and the mother of seven children, Molly Fumia is active in peace and justice issues and has written and lectured extensively on the challenges of world peace. She is a graduate of the University of Santa Clara and holds a master's degree in Theology from the Graduate Theological Union in Berkeley, California.

A *Child at Dawn* is her first book.

Permissions

Excerpts from *The Oath* by Elie Wiesel, copyright 1973. All rights reserved. Used with permission of the publisher, Random House, Inc.

Excerpts from *The Town Beyond the Wall* by Elie Wiesel, copyright 1964. All rights reserved. Used with permission of the publisher, Henry Holt and Company, Inc.

Library of Congress Catalog Card Number: 88-82702

International Standard Book Number: 0-87793-394-4

Cover and text design: Robert L. Mutchler

Printed and bound in the United States of America.

For Chuck

Acknowledgments

My sincerest thanks and love to my friends and family, for their unending and unbelievable support.

My special gratitude to Terry and Bob, for making the connections with me; to Missy, Mark, Nicholas, Gino and Kristen for their patience; to Helen for the gift of time; to Tom for being on my side; and finally to Mary Jane for lovingly naming my profession.

Contents

Foreword

This is a book about connections — unlikely connections. For what can a Jewish survivor of the Holocaust, who saw his faith and his family go up in smoke in a single night in upper Silesia, have in common with a woman raised comfortably and faithfully as a Catholic, now a mother of six?

Correction: Mother of seven: six alive, one who died after a week of life. Further correction: Jewish survivor who saw his faith and his family and six million fellow Jews go up in smoke. Elie Wiesel and Molly Fumia share at least the experience of death close at hand. There is a connection there.

But six million to one? Doesn't such a distance strain the possibility of connections? Of course it does. But death, which is no respecter of persons, is no respecter of numbers either. And in death's mysterious mathematics, the pain at the loss of a single child can be infinite, while the pain at the loss of six million lives can be . . . no more than infinite. This does not minimize by one jot or tittle the magnitude of six million deaths; it simply acquaints us more sensitively with the unbelievable magnitude of a single death.

Death by itself may not encourage connections. It may simply drive home more deeply the solitude of loss. But as

Molly Fumia discovered, since it was something Elie Wiesel had previously discovered, love encourages, and even builds, connections, and there is no way — as Pedro and Yehuda in Wiesel's novels remind us — to separate love and death. Frequently in our experience death seems powerful enough to negate the ultimacy of love, but on occasion love can wrestle death until the dawn and, like Jacob wrestling an angel, refuse to let it go without a blessing.

This book is such an occasion. It is Molly Fumia's testimony that the wrestling is worthwhile and that — *with help from another* — victories can sometimes be won over the power of death and the guilt that so often follows in its train. That she can share the pain of that struggle invests it with meaning for the rest of us, who, as recipients of her sharing, can begin to experience the love that enfolds it and is able finally to extract a blessing from it.

So here is the story of a stranger who entered Molly's life and became a friend. Because he too was sharing *his* pain, there could come out of it for her a bonding of love, and a liberation to move beyond personal suffering to find ways of forestalling the suffering of others.

I had the privilege of playing a small part in the story. I was the one through whom Molly first encountered Elie Wiesel. She didn't really need me after the initial introduction, so powerful were the chords of resonance that developed from her reading of him — rich, personal harmonies in the midst of the world's jangling discords. That such a thing happened once in the course of a lifetime of teaching would be sufficient vocational and personal reward. But I have been doubly blessed. For in these pages it is now the student who is speaking to the teacher, drawing me even closer than before not only to herself but to the one we both acknowledge as our common rebbe.

Robert McAfee Brown

Question Mark

"What is the death of a child?" Pedro asked.
"An injustice," I answered.
"No. That would be making a moral problem out
of it. It's more. It's a question mark."
(Elie Wiesel, *The Town Beyond the Wall*)

This is the story of what happened when Jeremy died
. . . and of what happened when I met Elie Wiesel. It is also
the story of what happened before I met Elie Wiesel, when
the death of a child was still a question mark.

I did not expect to become a storyteller. And I struggled with myself, and with Elie, over devoting so much attention to my own story when seen in light of his.

Here is a person, I often thought, who not only wit-
nessed the murders of most of his family and the people of
his village, but has, through the burden of memory, insisted upon witnessing the murders of six million other human beings, a million and a half children.

From the beginning, then, it seemed to me that my
suffering was so small in comparison. In my imagination, I
confided to Elie Wiesel this hesitation. Who am I to com-
pare a single, tragic moment in time to the loss of all hope,
and all humanity? In my imagination he smiled a slight

11

smile and pushed back the hair that flops on his forehead, a
bit frustrated, yet understanding. I believed that he would
speak not of comparisons, but of connections: To remember the past is to be more alive, more human in the present.
To connect one's personal human experience, one's small
sufferings, with all human experience, all suffering — it
is then, he might say, that we in our humanness will begin
to re-create the universe.

And so I found myself committed to a bold act. I used
one story to tell another. I found a familiar ghost among his
dead. I assumed that Elie wouldn't mind that I borrowed
his memory of the six million, of the one and a half million
children, to help me recall just one little boy. Finally, despite my hesitation, I welcomed that which was unexpected . . . it seemed that the journey through past and
present must disturb the conclusions of the future.

Admittedly, I am anxious to tell the ending of the tale.
But it is important to begin at the beginning, to call forth
the past. There is a story . . . . Like Elie's story, it begins
with remembering what happened, as precisely as possible, and then, going beyond the memory of the events, it
looks for meaning, and strives for truth. To find that meaning, I have employed one of Elie's literary techniques: a di-
alogue that transcends the actual events. And along the
way, I have interwoven his words, for his words have
helped to bring forth mine: the gift of life between storytellers.

I did not expect to give myself away, to Elie Wiesel or
anyone else. That I could be so influenced by the wisdom
and experience of another was a startling self-admission.
But in the end, it was I who was transformed by the giving
over.

Even after all this time, I am still moved, deeply moved,
by all that has happened. To say that I am thankful for this
journey might never be enough. But it will have to do.

The Story

Before the Death
of Childhood

> The tale the beggar tells must be told from the be-
> ginning. But the beginning has its own tale, its own se-
> cret.
>
> (Elie Wiesel, *A Beggar in Jerusalem*)

Whenever I remind Charles that he said he loved me on our first date, he doesn't remember doing it. How could anyone forget something like that? I remember. We had driven up to San Francisco. There we were, walking along the street, looking for where we had parked the car. He turned to me and said, "I love you." Just like that. And even though the setting was perfect for such an announcement, I didn't think it was romantic at the time. I thought it was pushy.

One time when we were laughing and arguing about that night, Charles insisted that I must have said I loved him too. But I didn't say it, not then. It was almost a year later, and again we were in San Francisco up on Nob Hill in a little park between Grace Cathedral and the Fairmont Hotel. We were swinging back and forth on a set of swings, and I told him that I loved him.

It was just about then that we began to imagine our-
selves as a team. Our choice for one another was easy and,
for me, an event that fearlessly opened up the future to
whatever might come along. My fortunes began with
Charles, as did my plunge into life's complexities.

At the time, my joy over our relationship was uncom-
plicated and expectant. He was, and still is, a very hand-
some man. He has dark olive skin, hair that is almost black,
and large brown eyes that are very expressive and always a
little sad. Even before we decided to get married, I thought
about how beautiful his children would be.

Just as Charles can't seem to recall our first date just as
it happened, he also denies having discussed the idea of our
having five children. But I remember. We were sitting outside a Chinese restaurant in San Jose. He said that his Aunt
Maxine and Uncle Frank had five children, and he thought
that was "about right." I was thrilled. I wanted lots of children, a large family like the one in my childhood fantasies.

As an only child, I spent many hours daydreaming
about what it would be like to have more people around. I
already had an extra bed; everything was ready for a sister.
When I was very small, I lived with two imaginary friends.
Later on, I often begged for friends to spend the night with
me, and when they did, I'd move the beds close to each
other so that we could talk and giggle long after we were
supposed to be sleeping.

But no one could come to my house on special nights
— like Christmas Eve. It was such a silly thought, spend-
ing Christmas Eve with a friend, but I imagined it anyway. Waiting for Christmas morning with a houseful of
brothers and sisters was one of my favorite fantasies.

A month after the movie in San Francisco and his dec-
laration of love, Charles invited me to his family's Christmas Eve gathering. I couldn't believe I had a date to
Christmas. My parents couldn't believe it either.

Charles' entire family — grandparents, aunts and uncles, cousins, as well as his parents, his two sisters and their families, and his little brother — welcomed me and the other "dates" (Charles has lots of cousins) as if we had always been part of the group. They were very lively, and loving, and also quite direct, as I caught snatches of arguments and confrontations going on as naturally as the warm Christmas greetings they were sharing. I wondered if this was the way big families were, so robust and unrestrained.

We got married on June 26, 1971, exactly one week after I graduated from college. Our family and friends toasted to our good health and to our many children to be. We raised our glasses while everyone cheered. I remember thinking, is that what comes next . . . our many children? I looked around at our closest friends. Nancy and Gerry had been married for a year and were anxious to start a family. Donna and Robert had been married two years longer, and were beginning to worry about the fact that they hadn't yet conceived a child. And Terry and Rick, whose wedding we would celebrate later that summer, had been laughing about how Terry might follow in her mother's footsteps and become pregnant quickly and quite often. Apparently the path before us had been determined.

Our friends and family toasted us, again and again, sending us on our way. At the time, it seemed so simple. The future was taken care of, the past could be easily abandoned. We were swirling around inside today, and it was, for the moment, glorious.

Charles and I returned from a month-long trip to Europe and rented an old, comfortable apartment not far from the college. On the day we moved in, we were greeted with an endless array of boxes and, to our surprise, Robert and Donna, who lived in an apartment below us.

So during those first few hectic months, when Charles was settling into his job with the family ranching business and I was back in college pursuing a teaching credential, we could share our new life together with others who seemed to be just a little ahead of us.

Donna was deeply concerned about not being pregnant. She and Robert were talking about taking some tests that sounded, at best, unpleasant. As for me, although having a child was not in my immediate plans, neither had I ruled out the possibility. Donna's fears unnerved me. Would we have similar troubles? How soon should we start trying, if only to prove that we were capable of becoming parents?

Meanwhile, Nancy and Gerry announced that their waiting was over. The telling seemed like half the fun; their first child was due in September. Gerry was pleased, but Nancy was, indeed, radiant. Suddenly her future was full of meaning, and she was completely ready for the baby's arrival within a few weeks of discovering she was pregnant. I couldn't help but share in her exuberance and decide, sometime during those days, that I wanted to have something just as exciting to tell and to feel those wonderful feelings too.

Our ambivalence toward family planning quickly paid off. In March of 1972, nine months after our wedding, Charles and I discovered that we were going to have a baby. By then, it seemed like a great idea. The family was excited, the grandparents ecstatic. It was fun to be pregnant: new clothes, new expectations, a name to choose, a room to ready. We moved into a small old house in downtown San Jose, and after finishing my teaching program in June, I settled down to a summer of waiting.

We went to childbirth classes where I learned to breathe deeply and Charles learned how to say, "You're doing fine." Still, I was afraid of the event. But then Nancy had her baby, a little boy named Gregory, and seemed to survive the pain we had worried about many times together. There was a baby shower; Nancy brought Gregory, who stole the show from the expectant mother. I wished that I had been first to deliver. Nancy was already thin and back to business as usual.

The baby was due on Halloween. I had thought that was a little odd, but of no real significance to our child. As the time drew nearer, I felt the glow of pregnancy disappear. My body strained to accommodate a large and active baby. I remember telling Charles that there were no words to adequately describe the last weeks of pregnancy. And I still had the delivery to look forward to.

October 31 came and went, but not without excitement. I stayed up all night waiting for Pasha, our German shepherd, to have her puppies. She worked very hard, but by morning she had delivered only two. At ten o'clock I phoned Charles; two more had arrived. By the time Charles came home that evening, there were eleven. At ten o'clock that night she delivered her last puppy, a stillborn male. I held him in my hand and observed his perfect features: He looked just like his brothers and sisters. Pasha had been too tired to push him through the birth canal quickly, and he had probably suffocated there while she struggled to bring him into the world. Pasha lifted her head and watched me while I wrapped her puppy up in a towel and carried him away. When I came back, she nudged me gently and gave up a little whine.

"It's okay, Pasha," I told her, "you've got enough babies." She seemed to contemplate my words, and then, exhausted, she put her head back down. I envied her. It was over and she could rest.

Two more weeks went by. The puppies grew and thrived, but I was losing interest in any babies other than mine. I was ready. All concerns about pain were overwhelmed by impatience. I was ready to have a child, at any cost.

Remembering the Week

> He burrowed in his memory, and searched care-
> fully. He turned pages, weighed episodes, examined
> the faces buried pell-mell in his depths. Finally he
> knew, from the trembling of his heart, that he had
> found what he wanted.
>
> (Elie Wiesel, *The Town Beyond the Wall*)

On the night of November 11, while celebrating Robert's birthday, I went into labor. I felt as though we were finally performing our parts in the play, after months of rehearsal. There was lots of laughing and worried looks, especially from the men, as I calmly finished my piece of birthday cake while everyone else timed my contractions. Charles' anxiety got us to the front door eventually, and after saying a hurried goodbye to the roomful of friends, we went home to pick up my long-packed suitcase, and to make sure that this was the real thing.

It was. My bag of water broke as we walked into the house; the contractions speeded up and intensified. Nevertheless, when we arrived at the hospital we were informed that we had a long night ahead of us.

I slept on and off as the hours wore on. Next door to me, a young Mexican girl screamed periodically in Spanish. A nurse came by, annoyed at my neighbor and unable to communicate any words of comfort, or scolding. I decided that I would not scream, no matter how much it hurt, so that the nurses would not talk about me to the other patients.

Finally, at about six in the morning, I began to progress. The nurses were full of praise, how brave I had been, how easy my delivery would be. I was pleased. This was working out fine.

Both my doctor and his partner were off duty for the weekend and another doctor whom I had never seen before came to say he would be delivering the baby. Dr. Simpson seemed nice enough, though a bit distant, and probably sleepy. He had been waiting for me all night. I felt bad about that.

The nurse came in with good news. I was ready for a caudal, the type of anesthesia that numbs the body from the waist down. While we waited for it to be administered, Charles and I congratulated each other on the ease with which we had met this challenge. I had done a great job; he had been a wonderful help. And now it was almost over. I wondered what the baby would be like. The caudal was given and the intense pain, which I had been controlling with the breathing exercises learned in class, slowly diminished to nothing. A nurse came in. She could see the baby's head; I was ready.

Once in delivery, I chatted with everyone, free of pain, feeling proud and excited, cooperating as much as I could. Charles came in dressed from head to toe in hospital garb. Underneath the surgical mask, I knew he was smiling.

The baby, a boy, arrived at 8:12 a.m., Sunday, November 12, 1972. Charles and I cried when our son cried for the first time. I held him for a moment, then the nurses insisted that he be taken away to be cleaned up and weighed. I fell asleep on and off while Dr. Simpson finished his post-delivery work. Someone came back with the news that the baby weighed eight pounds, 15 ounces.

"No wonder I have so much sewing to do," said the doctor. He looked up at me. "What's the baby's name?"

"Jeremy John Fumia," I said firmly. I loved that name.

When I arrived in my room in the maternity ward several hours later, the numbness had begun to wear off and with it my good spirits.

"It's your first and he was big. It's to be expected," explained the nurse attending to me.

The pain got worse and worse, and I felt that if I moved I would surely break in two. My head began to ache, another side effect of the caudal.

Charles came in with reports on how the news had been received by our families. Would I like to be the one to call our friends, Nancy and Gerry, or maybe Robert and Donna? I managed one phone call, but did not enjoy the telling because of the pain. Charles brought gifts, but they diverted my attention only momentarily.

Finally, at about eight o'clock, twelve hours after delivery, a nurse brought me my baby. I sat up painfully, but willingly, and reached for him. The nurse looked at me, a hint of exasperation on her face.

"This is your first? Well, we have a procedure."

One little foot protruded from the tightly wrapped blanket around the baby and on it was a hospital bracelet.

"These numbers must match," she demanded, grabbing my wrist band. When they did, she laid him on a sterile pad on the bed and undressed him for me.

I followed this activity with interest, nodding and murmuring my recognition of the fact that all of his parts seemed to be in order, flawless. I wondered if he was cold. It was, after all, November 12. She rearranged his little diaper and shirt and wrapped him back up.

"Watch out when you change his diaper. Little girls dribble, but little boys squirt." I grinned, not having thought of that.

"I see that you're bottle-feeding." She frowned, or was that my imagination? "Well, he might not take too much. Put him up on your shoulder and burp him after an ounce."

She handed the baby to me, and I responded with awkwardness. I tried to act naturally, making cooing noises at Jeremy while waiting for her to leave. But she was busy raising up the metal sides of my bed. She probably thinks I'll drop him, I decided. Finally, we were alone. He wasn't too interested in eating and seemed quite drowsy. We sat there together, but still separate. Maybe I should talk to him, I thought. Once when his eyes were open, I hoped that he was looking at me, despite what I had heard about babies not being able to focus for several weeks.

"Hello, Jeremy," I said. "Hello, Jeremy John."

He fell asleep and I put the bottle down beside me, hardly touched. I looked at my baby. His skin was olive, his hair brown. He had a cute little upper lip that poked out over a definite chin. Gently I took his hand. His fingers were long like mine. They moved a little as he slept.

After a while I noticed I was no longer concentrating on him. The pain of sitting up was almost too much to bear. Where is the nurse, I wondered, vaguely aware of the quiet and loving conversation that was going on between my roommate and her two-day-old daughter. I looked down at my son.

"Next time," I whispered to him, "I'll begin to know you."

Finally a nurse, a different one, came in to retrieve him.

"Did he eat?" she asked.

"Not really," I admitted, wondering if that was really okay.

"Don't worry," she smiled, aware of my insecurity. "Most of the time it takes them a while to get going."

They left, and I was reassured. He would eat next time. He would learn.

A nurse came in with painkillers. "Your doctor said you can have one of these every four hours." I felt protected. Everyone was taking care of me. "Do you want us to bring you your baby during the night? Or do you want to sleep?"

I wanted to sleep and escape the pain, but I didn't want to be a bad mother.

"You can bring him," I decided.

"Okay, we'll see you at midnight."

I slept soundly until the nurse turned on my light and gave me a washcloth to clean my hands and a sterile pad for my lap.

"Babies are coming!" she crooned as she swept through the room. I heard her words being echoed down the hall.

Jeremy didn't eat at all. I gave up after a few feeble attempts to interest him in the bottle of formula. I kept dozing off, waking each time with a start. My son slept peacefully in my arms. When the nurse came in, she woke both of us. I admitted that he had slept the entire time, and I asked for more painkillers.

"Would you like him at four?" My hesitation gave me away. "As long as you're bottle-feeding, maybe you should try to sleep until morning, dear," she said. "We usually feed the bottle-feds in the nursery during the night."

She had given me an out. I took it.

Monday morning. Jeremy is one day old, I thought. I felt better, and I was anxious for him to come. When they brought him in, his eyes were open and I decided to work hard at getting him to eat. He sucked a little bit, squirmed, even cried. I tried for what seemed like a very long time, becoming more and more uncomfortable. He didn't seem happy. Was he going to be a cranky baby?

"Come on, Jeremy," I said softly. "You have to eat." He didn't, and they took him away, leaving me alone behind the curtains that encircled the bed. I felt like crying, but didn't.

Later on, the baby's pediatrician came in. Steve Larussa was an old friend, my friend Nancy's father, and, of course, little Gregory's doctor, too.

"He looks fine, can't find a thing wrong with him," he reported.

We chatted together about other things. I was glad to see him.

"He's not really eating yet," I confided, trying, for some reason, to sound unconcerned.

"Give him time he'll be eating you out of house and home."

I smiled, reassured, although I had known his response before he said it.

The day continued with many visitors and more gifts. I walked, though painfully, to the nursery with the grandparents. All of their excitement and happiness came pouring forth in the same comments being uttered by other family members viewing their new arrivals.

"Look at that chin. He looks like his daddy."

"He looks just like Grandpa Fumia."

"He's beautiful, Molly, just beautiful."

Deep inside, a strong current of worry was beginning to thread its way through my entire being. I wasn't able to identify it; I only knew that I wasn't as happy as I should be. I decided that once I started feeling better, everything would be all right.

When visiting hours ended, I was glad to be alone. I

tried to write out birth announcements, but I stopped after two. I concentrated on the gifts, especially on a tiny football jersey with "Fumia" on the back that was hanging up on the curtain rod around my bed. I tried to imagine my son wearing it. I couldn't. I turned on the television.

That evening Steve Larussa came by again.

"The baby has a little fever."

I shivered involuntarily, as if waking up too fast. I swallowed. "Is that bad?"

"Well, I don't like it. It's only a hundred and one. That's not very high. I told them to call me, of course, if it goes higher."

If it goes higher . . . "What could the fever be from?" In an instant, terrible answers went through my mind. Why can't everything be all right?

"Did you have a cold when you came in?"

My throat had been slightly sore during the past week, as if I were fighting off a cold. Once in the hospital I had ignored it completely. I was suddenly uplifted by the possibility of an explanation.

"You know, I have been feeling like I'm coming down with something."

"Why don't you wear a surgical mask while you're feeding him? It's not good for an infant to be exposed to our infections."

So at the eight o'clock feeding, I wore a mask. While I waited for him to arrive, I thought about our situation. An infection from me. How long would I have to wear this mask? The nurse delivered my son to my arms. His eyes were wide open. I looked down at him. He probably wonders who I am. I felt like I couldn't communicate with him. I felt far away, less of a mother, more helpless.

I tried holding him in different positions, but none of them helped him want to eat. I was unhappy, nervous and self-conscious about the mask. There was nothing between the other babies and their mothers; it seemed like something big and unexplainable was between us.

The baby went back to the nursery. The tears finally came. I was frustrated, in pain, and worried. Charles called, understanding and reassuring, as always. The fever was probably nothing. Didn't I remember, that had happened to another baby of some friends of ours. Everything would be all right. Some sleep might help my "baby-blues."

I hung up the phone. Charles was right, of course. The fever was not unusual and probably not important. The mask was bearable if it would keep Jeremy from further infection. I shouldn't allow the mask to make me feel this way. It was just a thin piece of material, everything else was just the same as with the other mothers. I drifted off to sleep.

When the nurse came at midnight, I woke up quickly. I put the mask on, feeling refreshed, knowing that there would be a change. And he did seem hungrier. I kept holding up the bottle; he had taken an ounce. I put him up on my shoulder and patted his back. This is the way it will be, I thought. He will eat and I will pat his back. With his little head snuggling up to mine, I felt close and good. Daring further infection from my hand, I felt his forehead. He didn't feel warm. The fever was probably gone. Soon he dozed off, but I would have something to report to the nurse.

"Did he eat?" she asked methodically.

"Yes, over an ounce."

"Good. He hasn't been eating too much in the nursery, but we figure he's so big, he doesn't need to eat yet."

Was this the time I kissed him on the forehead? I don't think so; I allowed the mask to keep me from him. Beneath it, I smiled as the nurse picked him up. She looked at my son, and he looked back.

"Were you a good boy and did you eat for mommy?"
Just like all the other babies. "Say goodbye to mommy."

Was this the time I said, "Goodbye, Jeremy"? Was
there a glance, an instant that we connected? Did he feel
my hesitant, yet ever-growing love as we parted? The
mask, the mask. He couldn't have seen my smile as I
watched his little head disappear out of the room.

I would never hold him again.

Moments later, the nurse who had taken Jeremy away
returned.

"We won't be bringing him at four. We don't usually
bring the bottle-fed babies in the middle of the night. No
need to."

An objection, so slight I hardly noticed it, rippled
through me. There was a need, my need, but that secret
would remain unrevealed for years.

"And besides," she continued matter-of-factly, "he
has that fever."

I was disappointed, but I told myself that the eating
and the sleeping would help him . . . and me.

After nearly eight hours of sleep, I welcomed Tuesday
morning with optimism. I lay awake listening to breakfast
trays rattling and the clink of a mop against the furniture.
An old woman who always smiled her good mornings was
mopping my floor. Doctors came and went, talking and
laughing with the mothers. The maternity ward is a happy
place, I reflected to myself, different from the rest of the
hospital.

A head came around the corner of my door. "It's your
turn for a shower."

I went, unassisted for the first time, and stood there
for a long time enjoying the hot water on my bruised body.
When I got back to my room, my bed was freshly made and
a nurse was waiting for me.

"Will you be going home today?"

It had never occurred to me. It seemed too soon. And besides, the baby had a fever.

"I don't think so," I replied meekly. "My doctors haven't been in yet."

I got into bed and readied myself for the feeding. In the hall babies were whimpering. Was that Jeremy crying? He's probably hungry, I thought confidently. My roommate had gone home; the next baby to come into my room would be mine. I sat there, expectant, as footsteps came down the hall toward me. It was Steve Larussa.

He put his hands on his hips. "I think we'd better leave the baby in the nursery today." My spirits plummeted. "That fever is persisting, and we don't want to take any chances."

No, we don't, I thought dismally. "Can we still go home tomorrow?" I hadn't considered the possibility of going home without him.

"We'll see. We have to get that fever down." He looked sad. "I'll keep you posted."

I tried not to listen to the other babies being reunited with their mothers. I began to ache all over. My stomach hurt. I ordered more painkillers.

I called Charles with the latest development. He didn't say much; he would be by after lunch. A new roommate arrived, fresh from the delivery room, and I started to imagine what it would feel like when her baby came in and mine didn't.

During visiting hours, Charles and I walked down to see him. He was off by himself, so as not to infect the other babies. He was sleeping, a full bottle of water at the end of his little bed. Later, when visitors arrived, I took them down to see him in his lonely place at the end of the viewing window. My friends and relatives didn't seem too concerned, or perhaps they were hiding their fears from me.

Only my mother asked the questions that were rumbling around in my own heart.

"Well, what do they think it is, Molly? That doesn't seem right, a new little baby like that having a fever."

The whine in her voice annoyed me. "They don't know, Mother," I snapped. "They think he caught my cold."

She stood there, peering anxiously through the glass, indulging in concern. If she's going to get this upset, why doesn't she leave, I wondered cruelly. I turned away from her and walked back down the hall to my room.

The many trips to the nursery window took their toll. I couldn't wait for the painkillers to arrive at each four-hour interval. The babies came and went, and I sank into a stupor. I wanted the time to pass so that I would not have to feel anything.

A nurse came by to report. "The fever isn't too high, but we'll still keep him in the nursery for tonight." I didn't reply, and turned back to the television.

Charles came to eat dinner with me. I seem to remember walking down to see our son that night. The nurses arranged to open the curtains for us. He was sleeping, with a little frown upon his face.

"When can I pick you up tomorrow?" Charles asked cheerfully.

"I'll call you."

He left and I took my painkillers and went to sleep.

Wednesday. A whole lifetime in just one day. After breakfast I waited to be checked out by a doctor. I tried to guess who would be coming. I had not seen Dr. Simpson, who delivered Jeremy, since Sunday afternoon. My own obstetrician, Dr. Kara, had come in only once, very briefly, on Tuesday. It seemed he was supposed to be on vacation.

Dr. Kara's partner, Dr. Mancini, came in about ten

o'clock. He was much younger than Dr. Kara, who was white-haired, slightly built and soft-spoken. Vince Mancini had dark hair that rippled over his head and a pudgy stomach that, despite the best efforts of his belt, had escaped over his pants and outside his suitcoat. He was loud and friendly, directing the room as he entered it.

"Molly, you're all set. Everything's fine. I've ordered more painkillers for you to take home with you. Any questions?"

I liked him. He sounded so sure. Perhaps he could take control of the situation.

"The baby had a fever yesterday," I replied, "but I think we're still going home." It felt good to say that, and I wanted it to be true. Dr. Mancini only grinned, and before he left he congratulated me heartily on my recent motherhood.

A nurse came by. "Going home today?"

"I hope so."

"I'll go check it out for you," she offered. I was thankful. I wanted to be sure.

An aide came in and helped me pack. The hospital "gifts" were put in a large plastic bag. We laid out Jeremy's going-home clothes, which had been chosen months ago. I got caught up in the preparations and momentarily forgot the physical discomfort and my worries. I called Charles, confident that everything was normal, just like the other mothers and babies I had watched routinely departing for a new life together.

"Bring an extra blanket for the baby and pick me up at eleven." How nice it felt to take care of my son. This is the way it would be always.

I waited for the nurse to return. When she didn't, I began to notice the soreness once again. It intensified quickly, and making a place among all of our belongings, I sank back down onto the bed. I closed my eyes for a moment, and when I opened them again, a nun in full habit was standing at my door.

"Mrs. Fumia, this is for your baby boy." She handed me a small gold medal hanging from a tiny blue ribbon.

I took the medal and looked up at her. She seemed quite pleased with herself.

"God bless you, dear," she whispered. I didn't have time to respond before she was gone.

I examined the gift. It was familiar enough, a medal commemorating the Immaculate Conception of Mary, the mother of Jesus. She was standing on a cloud in her long flowing robes, halo above her head, radiating goodness. The words around her were almost too tiny to read, but it didn't matter; they were probably stored somewhere in my memory.

"Mary conceived without sin, pray for us who have recourse to thee," I recited absently. Turning it over in my hand, I decided the ribbons on the medals for baby girls were probably pink.

I thought about all the plastic statues and little medals I had received as a child for knowing my catechism lessons. I wondered where they were now. Perhaps up in a box in my mother's closet. Or maybe she threw them away.

The medal dangled from its ribbon in front of my eyes. Slowly I closed my hand around it, clutching it tightly. I could feel it coming. A long, silent wave of fear was pursuing me, then crushing me. A gift for Jeremy. The thought came and went without my holding it: *This is the only thing I will keep.*

Charles arrived and we waited. The nurse finally returned to inform us that Dr. Larussa was checking the baby out now and that she would bring him down as soon as he was finished. I nodded calmly, not wanting the normalcy of the moment to be cluttered with unnecessary words.

Finally, Steve arrived. I looked at his face and panic came racing back. Up to that time, and since then, I have never known him to be so serious.

"I think we should leave the baby here one more day. I want to have him checked out by another pediatrician."

We sat there, stunned. "Is the fever back?" I managed.

"The fever is low grade. I don't know what's causing it. If I let him go home, I'm afraid you'll just be right back in here." He hesitated. "I don't know, I just don't feel good about this."

I will never forget those last words. For years, I was grateful that Steve acted on his instincts. Since the baby didn't come home, I didn't get attached, I would say, and everyone would agree, knowingly. And the crib, and the clothes, and the stuffed dog we bought in Carmel just before I had him, what would I have done with all of that? They were never his. They would wait for the next baby. Everything would be all right. Much later, I wondered how I could have felt that way, and cursed Steve's instincts.

As we were leaving, a hospital volunteer came by with the customary birth photographs. I looked at the picture of my son, feeling like I didn't know who he was. I didn't buy them.

Many times afterwards I regretted that curious decision. When we tried to get the picture nine years later, the negatives had recently been discarded.

I sat in the wheelchair, holding my suitcase instead of my newborn. A nurse wheeled me down the hall while Charles walked beside me, the blanket he brought for our baby on his arm. As we sat waiting for the elevator, I thought about going to see him before we left. He would be all alone, far away from the other babies. The effort seemed overwhelming; I didn't say anything to Charles or to the nurse. Silence stared at the elevator doors.

I didn't cry until I walked into the house. My mother was there, standing in the living room, which was immaculate, like the rest of the house she had prepared for us. In the middle of the floor was the bassinet that Esperanza, a kind woman who worked for Charles, had made for us. I noticed how nicely the bassinet sheet stretched across the little mattress; there was a diaper laid out where his head would be, in case he drooled, I supposed. Another diaper was draped over the side of the little bed, folded perfectly. Everything was perfect. Everything except our baby.

I hurt all over, and I lay down on the couch, which would be my place for many days. Through the tears, I could see my father looking at me. He didn't say anything. I turned to my mother, who was trying to manage a smile in the face of disaster.

"They're just being cautious," she said matter-of-factly. "He'll probably come home tomorrow. You want him to get well, don't you?"

If only my wanting could help. I wasn't so sure he would come home tomorrow. I wasn't sure at all that he would get well. For a long time I said that I had known from the beginning. I never say that anymore.

I took my painkillers; my body was throbbing after the ride home. I dozed on and off, worried through the haze. Later in the afternoon Steve Larussa called. He and another pediatrician had determined that the baby's heart was enlarged. They didn't know exactly why. The baby would be moved by ambulance to the neo-natal unit at Valley Medical Center, where he could be attended by Dr. Carl Geraty, a pediatric cardiologist. I hung up, feeling like Jeremy was traveling farther and farther away from me. I didn't try to hold on. We won't be picking him up at the hospital tomorrow, I mused. If we go, he won't be there.

By six o'clock that evening, our baby was at the new

hospital. I couldn't imagine him there; it was a different place, unfamiliar. Eventually, I realized that I could no longer imagine him.

Carl Geraty called. His voice was low, soft, controlled.

"Mrs. Fumia, this is Dr. Geraty. I've just examined your baby." He took a little breath. "It doesn't look very good. We want to do some more tests."

He paused. I didn't say anything.

"I want to emphasize that this is very serious. You have a very, very sick baby."

I listened to the words. The baby was real, the baby was real and very, very sick.

"We want to do a cardiac catheterization. The baby has only a fifty-fifty chance of surviving this test." His voice continued to be soft and controlled. "We think we know what is wrong and the test will confirm it. As I said, if it is what I think it is, it is very serious."

"Will you do the test tonight?"

"Immediately, but we need your okay. Your baby won't feel much of anything, he'll be sedated. He won't be in any greater danger than he is now, really, and at least we'll know for sure."

"Will you call us?"

"As soon as I can, I promise."

I reported the conversation to Charles and my parents. No one said anything.

An hour later, Dr. Geraty called back. I was in our bedroom, sitting on the bed. Charles came in and stood there, watching me as I listened to the doctor's already familiar voice.

"The baby survived the cardiac cath." He took another little breath. "I'm afraid our suspicions have been confirmed."

He went on to explain the details and give the technical names. The baby had a congenital heart condition, hypoplastic left heart syndrome. The lower left ventricle was one-fifth the size it should be, and it contained only a few drops of blood. After he finished, I asked him what I needed to know.

"Are you telling me there's no hope?"

"Yes. It's terminal."

Silence on the phone. I wondered how quickly the waiting would be over.

"How long does it usually take?" I asked finally. If I let go now, would it be too soon?

"Maybe a day, maybe a week, a month. The longest I've seen a baby with this condition survive is two months. This is only the second time I've seen it. It's actually very rare. Most common in first-born boys."

My mind wandered for a moment. My next one won't be the first-born. Then I was jolted back to reality by the thought of two months of waiting. I hoped it wouldn't be that long. My immediate concern was that it be over quickly. How long would he be there, dying, while we waited? Charles left the room.

The doctor continued. "Mrs. Fumia, I don't advise you coming down here. If it were my wife, I wouldn't allow her to come. There's really no point. There's nothing you can do."

My mind jumped. The image of a woman, a child and a man between them rushed through my thoughts. There's nothing you can do. There's no point in coming. I wouldn't allow it. His words would echo in my head all week.

I hadn't thought about going or not going. Suddenly, I realized he was making it easy for me.

"Like I said," he repeated with even more emphasis, as if he knew he had my attention, "if it were my wife, I wouldn't allow her to come."

"You wouldn't?" I pretended to be deciding. I didn't

want to go, I couldn't. It would hurt too much. I wanted to
let go now, yesterday. Anyway, I shouldn't, the doctor
didn't advise it. He would call us tomorrow. I put the receiver down and stared at it. That's odd, I thought, just
yesterday we were worried about his having a cold.

I walked back into the living room. "It's terminal." I
returned to my place on the couch. My mother, leaning
against the door, uttered a little moan followed by deep,
uncontrolled sobbing. My father moved to comfort her.
Charles came and sat next to me and took my hand.

"I knew it," I insisted. I was moving past the present
as quickly as I could, running in slow motion, trying not to
notice what was passing by.

There was nothing to do but sleep. As I approached
our bed, I felt afraid. When I lay down, in the silence and
the stillness, would I have to think, would I have to feel? I
took my pills. Charles and I held each other and I began to
cry. Then it was morning.

Thursday. Charles' mother Catherine arrived early in
the morning. We talked a little; there wasn't very much to
say. But I was glad that she was there. For some reason, she
would make this day easier to bear.

I could hear her out in the kitchen, chatting with the
dog. Pretty soon Pasha escaped into the living room and
trotted over to see me on the couch.

"How's the mother?" I asked her, stroking her head.
She closed her eyes, happy for the attention. Only a few
more weeks, I thought, and all the puppies will have gone
to their new homes. Pasha will probably miss them.

I asked Catherine to take the dog back outside.

I thought of things to do. I became obsessed with the
need to talk to my own doctor, Dr. Kara. He didn't know,
and I must tell him what was happening. He would want
to know. I got his home number from a mutual friend and
left messages for him to call me. He finally called back later

in the morning and listened silently as I brought him up to date. He was very sorry. He would prescribe something for me, could someone pick it up? When we hung up, Catherine reminded me that he had recently lost a ten-year-old, the youngest of his eight children, to cancer. I was embarrassed. Maybe I shouldn't have bothered him at home. To lose a ten-year-old, compared to an infant that you barely know . . .

As the day progressed, the family members were notified and several of them called or came over. Dr. Geraty called. The baby was comfortable, eating a little, being taken care of in the best neo-natal facility around. How was I? Had my doctor prescribed something for me? Yes, Charles would pick it up this afternoon.

It was decided that Charles would go with his father, Johnny and sister, Janet, to see the baby that evening. I sat on the couch and took this news apprehensively. Should I go too? I was afraid of the answer. Charles reassured me that I shouldn't go if I didn't feel up to it. Inside I hoped I would never feel up to it. If he was still alive next week, there wouldn't be a reason for me not to go. But Dr. Geraty wouldn't allow his wife that pain. It must, indeed, be a terrible thing to see one's dying child. I took the pills that Charles brought home and more painkillers.

While Charles, Janet and Johnny went to Valley Medical Center, I stayed on the couch and waited. Hazy images tumbled about my mind, without consideration, without my permission.

They are at the hospital by now. They are moving closer. Soon he will be there, in front of them. They will have to look.

Johnny will not be afraid. He watched his younger brother, Charles, while he was dying. He looked into his face, too young for death, while he lay in his casket.

Even now Johnny grieves for his beloved Charles. I

have always wondered about that. I have never known a wound that didn't seem to heal, even a little . . .

My mind slowed down, my body relaxed. I stared out the window at the trees in the front yard. It was dusk. Each small pane of glass was a perfect rectangle. The leaves on the trees were brown and yellow and red, and falling as I looked without seeing. Charles' blue Ford was parked in its usual place next to the curb. My eyes moved from the trees to the leaves, to the black wrought-iron railing next to the steps of our front porch and back to the trees. The bark on the biggest tree was uneven and chipping away like the paint on the house next door.

Across the room my mother and Catherine sat nervously on the loveseat. My mother had been going in and out of the kitchen, waiting for me to use a glass or a dish so that time could be spent washing it, drying it and putting it away. Catherine had stayed in the living room, standing only a few feet away from me, looking through the basket of cards that we had received since Jeremy's birth. But now the dishes were done and all of the cards had been read. The scene seemed almost comical. There they were, the two of them, squeezed together on the loveseat while I stretched out on the long couch. Once in awhile, someone would say something, but I didn't really listen.

Suddenly my mother gave a little shriek and jumped up. She had burnt a hole in the loveseat with her cigarette. She apologized profusely and scurried about, trying to undo the hole, I imagined. Didn't she know that from now on, the hole would always be there?

Catherine wept a little, dabbing her eyes with a Kleenex. Much later, I believed that she was feeling the pain for all three of us. My mother was focusing on my suffering, wondering how I could be so brave. She didn't know I wasn't feeling anything.

For the moment, I was a spectator. The numbness

moved me in and out of indifference. I talked about how I would have an angel in heaven, and reminisced about how God had been preparing me for this in the hospital.

Was it only Catherine who had entered the darkness, and who had begun to grieve for Jeremy?

When they arrived home, Janet and Johnny were devastated. I sat up, alert, as Charles dropped down on the couch next to me. He began to cry.

"It's my fault, it's my side of the family." Charles has a slight heart condition and was willing to take the blame. Instantly, I was holding him, telling him firmly that it was a chance thing, as the doctors had said, and nothing genetic. He calmed himself and told me about their visit.

"When we got there a nurse was holding him, rocking him in a rocking chair." I began to tremble all over. "I held him and rocked him, too." Janet had held him, and Johnny, dear Johnny. My world came crashing in around me, as the image of my husband holding his dying son forced its way into my consciousness.

"Was he awake?" I whispered, struggling to hold on.

"Off and on. His eyes would open and then he would go back to sleep. I think they've got him sedated."

Each question and each answer was like a dagger in my heart. "Is he eating?"

"Yes, a little." Still trying, little Jeremy. It's no use.

Everyone was crying. He's still alive, he's real, I thought. He's not gone yet. He opens his eyes, he eats a little.

Pain engulfed me. After a while, the incessant tears flooded in to wash away the images that were causing them.

Night had descended into the room, but no one bothered to turn on a light. We sat there, together, in the darkness and the silence. There was nothing more we could do; we knew that now, convinced, finally, by Janet and

Johnny and Charles, who were witnesses. And yet, a small hope seized me: Was there still one more way that I could care for my son?

"Charles," I noticed that my voice seemed to startle everyone. "He hasn't been baptized. We must call a priest, maybe one of our friends . . . ."

Charles' hand on mine stopped me.

"I called for the hospital chaplain," he said gently, "and he baptized him." My husband paused, and I looked into those beautiful brown eyes, now dulled with sadness and pain. "I'm sorry, Mol, I don't remember his name."

And so I resigned myself to the finality. Whoever this priest was, I hoped, he must have known that my baby's name was Jeremy.

Eventually it was time for bed. I took my pills. Charles and I held each other again, talking. I began to sob. I wanted so much to let go, of something. Finally, I heard my own voice crying out, "I want my baby! I want my baby!"

The sound echoed inside of me, crashing again and again against the fragile walls of my faltering spirit. Oh God, I thought, I can't stop it anymore. I'm breaking apart.

Charles held me for a long, long time. Eventually, the voice dimmed, and the walls stopped crumbling. I succumbed to the numbing effect of the drugs, and to the more ancient opiate of exhaustion.

On Friday morning, Charles went to work for a while. I didn't want him to go, but I knew it would give him something to do. He promised that he would take me for a ride in the afternoon. I looked forward to moving away from the couch, the rectangular window panes, the falling leaves.

We drove across town to see Robert, who owned a bakery. Charles left me in the car and went into the building. Soon they emerged together, walking slowly toward me, Charles talking, Robert listening. When they got to the car, Robert hugged me and admitted that he could not believe the truth. I told him that I felt bad because the baby was born on his birthday. It would have been so nice.

Later that evening, Robert brought Donna to see me. In the haze of those days, a few things stood out. Donna's visit was one of them. Apparently she had insisted on the visit immediately, terribly upset but determined to do what she had to do. She rushed through the front door and was in tears before she sat down next to me on the couch. We cried together.

"I can't believe it," she said over and over. I observed that she wasn't at a loss for words like most everyone else. After a while she put her hands on my shoulders and looked me squarely in the eyes.

"Molly, we're going to do this together. You're not going to be alone; I can't believe this has happened, but it has, and we're going to make it, together."

I remembered that Donna's father had died only a few months earlier. Had someone said those words to her? *Comfort* They were so comforting. She was so sure. We would do whatever we had to do together.

Each day Dr. Geraty called and said the same thing. The baby was getting weaker, but was not uncomfortable. He didn't think that it would be too long. I hoped not. Once more he assured me that I shouldn't come down to the hospital. There was nothing I could do. I wanted to believe him. Inside, I felt a vague sense of relief, but I wished that he wouldn't talk about it. What would everyone think, if they knew?

On Saturday I took my pills and waited. Charles' grandmother came by. I was surprised to learn that she had gone to see her great-grandson. I worried about who else had gone. Maybe they weren't telling me.

"He's just beautiful. It's too bad." She tried and failed
to hold back the tears. She and I exchanged a glance. How
many times I had listened to the stories of her own life as a
young mother, a story now two generations past. And
now, in that glance, her eyes were filled with the wisdom
of experience and understanding. She knows, I thought to
myself. She knows so much more than I.

That night Nancy and Gerry came by, leaving Gregory with her mother. Nancy told me that when her father
had broken the news, he had cried. She said that all she
could do was run to hold Gregory close to her. She must
love her son so much, I thought.

Later we talked about Jeremy as an angel in heaven.
Jeremy would be our link to forever. Nancy laughed typically and said, "Little Jeremy-mia." She had concocted a
nickname for someone who would never be. After that,
there was an awkward silence.

Rick and Terry, the couple we had asked to be the baby's godparents, joined the gathering. Soon everyone was
laughing and things seemed quite normal. In the middle of
a conversation, I decided I was tired and went to bed. Was
I acting strangely, I wondered, when I abruptly said goodnight and left the room? It didn't matter.

Daybreak. My eyes follow the Angel of Death . . .
My lips begin to whisper on their own: I don't under-
stand, I don't understand, no I shall never understand.
(Elie Wiesel, *The Oath*)

Sunday. Has it only been a week? Catherine came
over early; my mother had stayed through most of the
week, quietly making sure our house was in order. At
about eight-thirty the phone rang. As I picked it up, I knew
that Jeremy was no longer real. Oh no, I thought, I can
wait longer, let him be real a little longer.

"Mrs. Fumia, this is Dr. Geraty." His voice seemed to catch. I could hardly hear him. "The baby died about a half hour ago."

His name is Jeremy, I thought. Doesn't Dr. Geraty know his name?

"There was no discomfort, no pain."

My mind went slowly. He lived exactly a week. That's quite a long time, long enough to be a real person. But it's over now. He was, and now he isn't anymore. He isn't opening and closing his eyes. He isn't trying to eat or moving his long fingers. He isn't squirming or crying. His little heart isn't trying to be right anymore. All the things I knew about Jeremy had ceased to be.

"What do parents usually do, Dr. Geraty?"

He still spoke softly, but his tone was more business-like. "Well, we would like your permission for an autopsy. In two or three weeks I would like you and Charles to come in and we'll talk. Let's give it that much time, though."

He remembered Charles' name. Hadn't anyone told him Jeremy's name?

He continued. "Parents do different things. Some go for the whole funeral, open casket, the whole bit." Of course we wouldn't do that. Had he lived long enough, was he real enough for a funeral? "Others choose cremation. There are a lot of things in between, I suppose."

I had been thinking about cremation. It seemed appropriate.

He said how sorry he was and I believed him. We hung up, and I stood and moved reluctantly toward the door of our bedroom, stopping when I saw myself in the mirror above my dresser.

"Oh God," I murmured weakly, staring at my own face and wondering what I would do next. But the reflection just stared back, defeated, until I didn't want to look anymore.

My eyes dropped down to the dresser. The little medal with the blue ribbon I had been given in the hospital was resting on top of my jewelry box. I tried not to lose control. What happened to my baby? He must have been here once, I told myself, grasping the medal. This wasn't here when I left to go to the hospital. Surely this is a sign that something is different. I stood there for a few moments, waiting for the confusion to recede and my body to stop trembling. *This is all that is left, and I will keep it always.* I tucked the medal away in the bottom of the jewelry box and went into the living room, where Charles, Johnny and Catherine, and my own mother and father were waiting.

"He's gone," I choked, the tears beginning to flow again, unrestrained.

Charles was there quickly. "Now, Mol," he said gently. "We knew it would happen. It's better this way."

I composed myself, believing he was right. We started to discuss the arrangements. Charles and I wanted to have a memorial Mass that night at the university chapel.

Catherine, who had been silent, began to think aloud. "That's pretty fast. How will we tell everyone, and besides, the baby won't be ready."

I reacted violently. "The baby won't be ready! What are you thinking of?" I demanded. No one can look at my baby anymore. I can't look. When I mentioned cremation, she lost control.

"You just can't cremate that beautiful little boy." She was beside herself, disbelieving. Her words annoyed me, but I decided that she must not understand. I understood. His spirit was all that mattered, and that was with God.

"What do you want, Catherine?" I asked her wearily, struggling to focus.

"It's not what I want," she was suddenly gentle, "it's what you want, of course. It's just that I thought we'd have a little service, something simple, something so that everyone can come. And they don't all have to go to the burial."

I couldn't keep up with her. What I want, I thought miserably, is for this to be over.

They continued to talk, but I knew I would no longer be safe if I stayed there with them. So I retreated further behind the wall of haze that was there now, whenever I needed it, protecting me from losing myself, from exploding with desire.

The waves of feeling subsided. Catherine doesn't understand. The ashes can end our waiting.

Charles' voice called me back to reality. How would it be if he called an old friend, a mortician, to talk about our alternatives? He made the call in the other room, and was back in a few minutes. While he was gone no one said a word.

He sat beside me and took my hand. "Joe says he'll arrange to get him from the hospital and they'll use a little pine box — no embalming or anything like that. We can bury him in a plot in the children's cemetery."

Grateful tears flowed down Catherine's cheeks, and I sensed that we were all satisfied. There would be no service at the cemetery, only the memorial Mass that night. Later, maybe in a few weeks, Charles suggested, maybe then we could go to the cemetery. I didn't think it mattered if we ever went.

On the way to the Mass, I thought about death. Dying is different, I decided, than anything I had ever imagined. Gone was the dark cloud of unknowing, and the familiar bursts of panic and fear. Instead, we were somehow inside of death, Jeremy and I, and we weren't afraid of beginning, and ending, and continuing.

If only we could stay here, I thought. If only I could remember this feeling, this connection with something so pure and true. My son, who had been behind me, just be-

ginning the journey, had rushed by quickly, moving ahead
to a new place filled with wisdom. Dear God, I prayed, let
this child lead me through life's secrets, and give meaning
to everything that is meaningless.

It hurt to walk, so I slowly shuffled down the hallway
to the chapel on Charles' arm. Our friends and family had
spent a busy afternoon. The chapel was packed with people. Friends, relatives and even a few people I didn't know
looked at me; I felt as though I was inside a bubble, and I
couldn't touch them. Many people were crying, and I wondered what they were feeling. I couldn't comprehend the
intensity of the emotions that were making the room swell
and sway back and forth. I believed, through the now familiar fog that prevailed, that something good was happening.

The "Mass of the Angels" was celebrated. I waited for
the priest, an old friend, to say Jeremy's name. He did,
once, or so I thought, but then he seemed to forget. He
called him "the child" or "this little one."

As the end approached, I leaned over to Charles and
whispered, "Don't you think we should say something,
thank all these people for coming?"

Charles stood up and began to talk softly to the gathering. I watched him, wondering how deeply he was hurt-
ing. Most of the attention had been on me. Had he had
time to grieve? My eyes moved to Charles' father, sitting on
the other side of him. Love and grief. Johnny had started to
cry, a gentle, loving father watching his first-born son
thanking people for coming to celebrate the life and death
of another first-born son. I was hypnotized by his pain, and
by the profound love I was witnessing, knowing it was special, and something to be cherished and remembered by all
of us, sons, daughters and grandchildren of this wonderful
man.

Charles stopped and I stood up and took his arm.

"Yes, thank you everyone, from the bottom of our hearts."
I didn't know what else to say. After a moment I added,
"Please don't worry about us, we'll be all right."

The Mass ended and nearly everyone came over to
talk to us. I smiled at each of them, receiving their em-
braces, wondering if I had been presumptuous. Maybe
they weren't worrying about us. Maybe they were thinking
about Jeremy. I wished that I had said something else.

Many people came by the house afterwards. There
was drinking and eating and laughing, until finally everyone thought to leave us alone. I wasn't sure that I wanted
them to go; again, I was afraid of the silence of the night in
our bed. I took my pills. *Denial? of Grief*

We held each other, as we had every night since the
nightmare began. I stared into the darkness. What would I
do tomorrow? Thoughts of my baby, once warm in my
arms, opening and closing his eyes, now lying cold and still
somewhere in the night, began to creep in. There were a
few tears, one here, one there. I worked hard not to think
or to question. Most of all, I didn't ask if anyone was holding him when he died.

I knew that if I held off the feelings long enough, sleep
would take over. It did.

The next morning Jeremy John Fumia was buried under number 62 in the children's cemetery. No one was
there.

Breaks in the Silence

> Happy are those who close their eyes: for them nothing changes.
>
> (Elie Wiesel, *The Town Beyond the Wall*)

I am not sure when I first knew how wrong everything had been.

There were, for sure, some moments of initial recognition, some breaks in the silence. But for the most part, almost six years came and went without questions, much less answers. And all the while, the wounds remained open, unattended, unhealed.

There were a few times when my heart, longing for understanding, tried to alert me to consciousness. I remember especially the day after he died. My mother had arrived early in the morning to help out with the house, and just to be there for me, a ritual that would be repeated many times during the weeks it took me to recuperate. We were standing together in the bathroom, in front of the mirror. Was that really me staring back, looking so tired and pale? And then the image turned fuzzy.

Silently I reached for the bottle of pills that had been prescribed for me. My mother read the label over my shoulder: Valium. We watched together as I poured them down the toilet. I became determined to heal physically, and to start my life again.

Later that day, Dr. Kara's office called. Had I ever had the German measles? My mother was sure that I hadn't. The nurse said that I should have an injection, right away if possible, so that I would not have to worry about the dangers of German measles during my next pregnancy.

My next pregnancy. Yes, that was all in the world that I wanted. We could give the new baby Jeremy's room, because I hadn't brought him home. I was so thankful. It could have been so much worse.

My mother drove me down to the office.

"Of course you understand," the nurse told me as she was preparing to give me the injection, "that you cannot become pregnant again for at least three months. This injection is the same as giving you a case of the German measles, and it is in the first three months of pregnancy that this disease almost always produces a deformed child."

I didn't want to wait three months. I added up all those months of waiting that had already passed and were still to come. What would I do all that time? The nurse walked toward me, smiling. I wanted to tell her we'd take our chances with the German measles.

"All finished," she said to me cheerfully.

Too late, I thought, fighting off a sense of panic. The nurse didn't say anything about my baby who had died the day before. Before I left the office, she handed me a prescription for three months' worth of birth control pills.

Six weeks later I went to see Dr. Kara for the regular post-partum check. I was anxious to see him, willing to talk. And I did talk, felt some things, cried a little. He wrote on my chart, listening intently. Then he turned to me, smiling an empty smile, his hand on the doorknob.

"You'll have lots of babies." Then he left.

The next day Dr. Kara's partner, Vincent Mancini, called me to tell me that he would like to be my doctor. I wondered if Dr. Kara didn't want me anymore. And again I was reminded of his own dead ten-year-old son, and I knew that he must resent my grief over a week-old infant. Gratefully, I accepted Dr. Mancini's offer.

Exactly seven months after Jeremy's death we discovered that a second baby was on the way. Everyone rejoiced at the news, and I hoped that soon everything would be made right again. Dr. Geraty had assured us that the odds were in our favor, and that there was every reason to believe that our future offspring would be healthy and normal.

I worried a little anyway. But not as much, apparently, as everyone expected me to. I already had Jeremy, and now I would have a second baby. Even though Jeremy was not there, I had decided somehow that things were as they should be. My struggle was not with my fears, but with our friends.

During those months of waiting, it seemed like every woman I knew had a baby. Baptisms and baby showers dotted our calendar. Jeremy's godparents asked us to be the godparents of their new son. Now and then I was jealous of the happiness of our friends, and I resented how easily they produced healthy children.

And sometimes, as I watched the new mother delighting in her infant, I would warn her silently: *Don't think you are ahead of me. I was a mother before you.*

I stubbornly insisted on fitting in with the other new mothers. In the fall of 1973, when I was six months pregnant, we joined a large group of friends for a picnic at a nearby park. Nancy and Gerry were there with one-year-old Gregory. Terry and Rick brought our godson, Jason. Our old friends Robert and Donna were happily spreading the news that their first child was due in February.

Some of the women sat in a group, chatting about pregnancy and delivery while a few toddlers played at their feet and new babies slept in their arms. It was a familiar scene: young mothers comparing notes on the harrowing experience of bringing a child into the world.

"When those pains really started to come," Nancy laughed, "I forgot everything they'd taught me. The problem then is just to survive!"

I smiled at my friend. She is so wonderfully honest, I thought. Another friend of ours, Maryanne, who was expecting her first child any day, revealed some of the familiar fears even while she was trying to sound confident.

"I'm glad David will be there with me." She glanced over at her husband, who was cooking hamburgers with Charles and Robert. "We've practiced a lot. I'm sure he'll remind me of what I'm supposed to do."

Nancy looked at me and rolled her eyes. "I hope David doesn't get stuck in traffic," she remarked. Even Maryanne laughed.

At that point I spoke up about our delivery, the way my labor had begun, how I had felt, how Charles had helped. David wandered over to our group while I was talking. When I had finished, he addressed me softly, but with a voice that was stern and demanding.

"Molly," he began, putting his arm around Maryanne as if to protect her from me, "can't you see how scared she is? It would be better if you didn't say those things to her."

I stared at him. What things? That I went into labor? That Charles was there? That we delivered our child?

Anger and embarrassment engulfed me. I turned and walked away as fast as I could, in no particular direction, stopping only when I reached the grass by the lake.

No one understands. They can't change what has happened. I am a mother and no one can take that away.

Charles caught up with me and I threw myself into

his arms. After a moment, he held me back from him, searching my face, his own etched in concern. Tearfully, I related the conversation.

"He's afraid, too, Mol," he told me solemnly. "He probably didn't mean anything. He just doesn't want Maryanne to worry."

"Charles," I protested, "anything can happen, you know. Once you're pregnant, you're vulnerable. Things don't fit together perfectly anymore. They'd better wake up."

We went home without saying goodbye to anyone. I waited all evening for David to call and apologize. But instead, they went to the hospital to have a beautiful, healthy baby girl.

> I should have liked to know this little brother, both younger and older than myself. Whom did he resemble? My mother?
> (Elie Wiesel, *The Oath*)

Vince Mancini delivered our second child, Melissa Ann, on January 3, 1974. I had a cold when I delivered. I did not wear a mask while I nursed her, and she did not get my cold.

For the next three days, my hospital room was a madhouse. A constant flow of family and friends came to congratulate us and see our healthy daughter. Charles took armloads of flower arrangements and gifts home after each of his visits. Telegrams arrived from various parts of the country and the phone never stopped ringing. Finally, a thoughtful nurse took my phone off the hook and closed the door when she found my room momentarily empty.

"I think you're breaking the record for baby celebration," she remarked as she cleared away two empty champagne bottles from the night before. "Where did these come from?" she laughed.

I tried to explain. "You see, our first baby died. And everyone is very excited about Missy being healthy. They want to share the joy with us. This is the payoff, I suppose, for sharing the pain."

Even though I could explain it to the nurse, I was inwardly amazed by the outpouring of happiness that was going on around me. Two months after Missy came home, we baptized her in the same chapel where we had celebrated Jeremy's short life. Afterwards, the christening party was held at Johnny and Catherine's house.

With Missy in my arms, I moved from room to room, trying to talk to each of more than a hundred guests. Planning this party had been like planning another wedding. Besides all of our friends and the entire family on both sides, Catherine invited many of their old friends, all of whom had been there the night we had Jeremy's Mass. Then there were new friends, neighbors who had shared our misfortune, and others who had touched our lives and were somehow connected to the wonderful conclusion of these 14 months of waiting.

It took two hours to open the gifts, but no one seemed to mind. We ate and drank and sang and danced long after Missy was safely tucked away in a crib in Charles' old bedroom.

Later, when everyone except our closest friends and family had gone, Johnny brought out an old and treasured bottle of wine and handed it to his son.

"Open it, Charles," he commanded, "and we will drink one more toast together to Melissa Ann Fumia.

We all raised our glasses and cheered the sleeping infant, and the room and that night were enveloped in love, and in hope for the future.

The future developed quickly. Mark Joseph was born on July 26, 1975. Like his sister, he was delivered without anesthesia, and nursed until he was eight months old.

Everyone was glad to have another baby boy, a healthy little heir. From what I could remember, Mark didn't look at all like Jeremy; he had fair skin and blond hair. Having a girl and a boy was nice, I told myself. If I still had Jeremy, one of these children may not have come along. I felt more complete than I had in a long time. And when we again celebrated the birth of our healthy son with a rousing christening party, I felt a happiness that was indescribable.

> The question remains open and no new fact can change it.
> (Elie Wiesel, *A Beggar in Jerusalem*)

I developed a way of dealing with Jeremy's memory. I understood only vaguely that I had some needs where he was concerned, and I struggled to fulfill them without ever asking where they came from or what they meant. When I was pregnant with Mark, I would always explain to anyone who asked that this would be my third child. Invariably, they would pursue the conversation, wanting to know if I had one of each sex, their ages, their names, and I would then have to add, "We lost our first little boy."

This conversation reoccurred often. My questioner would always be made to feel sad and embarrassed, which sometimes satisfied me, sometimes distressed me. And to say that we had "lost" a child was never quite right. Did we lose him, or did he die, or both?

One thing was clear. I was obsessed with his name. Jeremy John. I loved to say it. It was my way of identifying his reality. He really existed; I have another son, I would insist to myself.

His name seemed so important. Catherine understood about names. When she had her first son, she insisted that he be named Charles John, in order to remember Johnny's brother. Then, 15 years later, they named their second son John Charles. Many of their friends teased them, sure that they had somehow gotten stuck. But it wasn't that at all. She understood that each of those names must be remembered, celebrated and carried on. They must never be lost or forgotten.

In May of 1976, when Mark was ten months old, I discovered that a fourth child would arrive the following February. Since Jeremy, each pregnancy had been proclaimed a great blessing. But this time my enthusiasm was tempered a bit by the thought of three babies only three years apart.

To make matters worse, no one seemed to view pregnancy the way I did. They said things that confused me and made me angry.

For instance, one day a friend of mine casually asked why I would want another child when I already had a boy and a girl.

"I suppose we have to break the tie," I snapped.

She laughed uneasily, but I continued to glare at her, thinking about how much she had to learn, and about how for us the tie was already broken.

What is happening to me, I asked myself as that moment passed. What else is there? But the answers were still years away.

In August I miscarried at about 14 weeks. The experience was horrible. Two weeks of bleeding, wondering, not knowing what to pray for. I finally "spontaneously aborted" the baby late on a Friday afternoon in Dr. Mancini's office. The next week, when I went back in to see him, we talked about the miscarriage. I don't recall how the conversation started, only how it ended. I had become enraged.

"Do you remember?" I demanded, aware of the fact that my voice was rising and the door to his office was wide open. I slammed my hand down on the examination table.

"I was lying right here, blood all over me. Your nurse was annoyed that I had made such a mess. So I apologized. I apologized!"

"You shouldn't have done that, Molly. It wasn't your fault."

"She didn't seem to think so, Vince. She accepted my apology."

I stared at him, but he didn't say anything. He wasn't willing, I suppose, to challenge my version of the events.

"Don't you remember, Vince? Here I was, tears streaming down my face, mourning for my baby that you insisted on calling an embryo."

I paused for a moment, watching him, not caring how much what I was saying might hurt him.

"But you didn't notice," I continued, allowing my anger to choose the words, "because my blood and what was left of my child had clogged up your sink."

Color drained from his face. He was crushed. I was surprised. I went home wondering if there were other things I needed to feel and say. For the moment, I had said enough.

I decided to take a break from having children. I had expended so much energy in having them, and in losing them, that big pieces of my life had been neglected or forgotten.

Missy and Mark delighted me, yet I felt restless and incomplete. I went on a retreat to attempt to weave the various strands of my life, which seemed to be waving aimlessly about, back together.

Gradually, I rediscovered my spiritual self, and I came to appreciate the small moments I found for quiet meditation in the middle of my noisy days. It was for me an exciting time of spiritual exploration. Through prayer, I began seeing things differently, connecting what I could glimpse of the spiritual universe with the rather terrifying signs of our times. I felt more whole, more alive than I had in a long while.

Inevitably, my long-standing social and political concerns were rekindled by that newly empowered spirit. Taking the children along with me, I plunged into social activism. I became more involved with the poor in our area, and we all helped out at the local soup kitchen and shelter for the homeless. I studied the connections between poverty and militarism, and attended gatherings which deplored both. I joined other Catholics who were striving to integrate spirituality and work for justice and peace in their lives, and found in those communities some extraordinary individuals and lifelong friends.

Charles was not about to become a social activist. But our conversations were again sprinkled with questions of politics and economics as well as Missy's progress at nursery school or Mark's tangles with the little boy next door. He tried hard to be supportive and helpful as I juggled the various parts of my life to fit into days that were only 24 hours long.

Somehow, the children kept up with me, and I with them. Our lives together were turning out differently than either Charles or I had imagined, yet it seemed that we were being beckoned forward . . . promised a way to make it all work.

During those days, life became fuller and faster. There was no time for remembering.

> The living person I was, the one I thought myself to be, had been living a lie; I was nothing more than an echo of voices long since extinguished . . . I thought I was living my own life, but I was only inventing it.
> (Elie Wiesel, *A Beggar in Jerusalem*)

It happened about a year after my confrontation with Vince Mancini. I was at a church with a group of people I didn't know very well. We were talking, sharing with each other the single experience in our lives that had most affected our faith. I talked about Jeremy, about how he had helped me feel close to God and unafraid of death. I talked about knowing him only for a week, and what a gift that had been. Everyone was moved, and impressed with my ability to transcend the loss of a child and emerge with renewed faith. One person, a young man, reflected the thoughts of the group.

"Really living life to the fullest sometimes means being with those we love in death. In that short time, your son had a wonderful mother."

The smile that I had been directing toward him froze on my face. Over and over again, shocking words of accusation penetrated my being: *It didn't happen that way. That's not what happened. You lied.*

I drove home trembling. To my horror, the days of that week so long ago came into focus. The hazy dream became a nightmare. I pushed it away. It pursued me. *You never knew him. You didn't see him after Tuesday. You didn't hold him after Monday.* I walked into the house where my two small children were playing. He was a person, a human being just like them. Who would he have been? *You never knew him. You could have known more; there were five more days between the last time you saw him and the day he died. It's different than the way you tell it. You weren't a good mother in the short time you had. They only think you were. You lied.*

I picked up little Mark and held him close to me. Gradually my heart stopped pounding; the feelings faded away. By the next day, life appeared to have slipped back into the ordinary.

But something had changed. There was to be no further retreat into oblivion. The illusion was in danger, the numbness had been pierced.

God of my childhood, show me the way to myself.

(Elie Wiesel, *The Town Beyond the Wall*)

After a break of three and a half years, I gave birth to
Nicholas John on December 7, 1978. The pregnancy had
been rocky; I almost miscarried and was confined to the
couch for many weeks. When he finally arrived, perfect
and beautiful, a brown-haired, olive-skinned little boy, I
decided that God and I were now even.

It would take still another pregnancy to bring me
back to center stage with my first-born son.

More than seven years had passed since Jeremy's
death. It was the spring of 1980. From the very beginning
of this new nine months of waiting, I was aware of a
strong, yet unspoken sense of alarm that I was carrying
around with my unborn infant. I was much more worried
about the health of this baby than I had ever been while I
carried Missy, Mark or even Nicholas, whom I had almost
lost. Why, I asked myself, after three healthy children, am
I convinced that this child would not be all right?

And there was something else going on. As the baby I
carried came to life, every kick signaled a warning: The
memories were there, gathered at the edge of my consciousness, waiting to be called forth to testify.

On several occasions, the silence was broken. We
would begin to talk, Charles and I, or once with Johnny
and Catherine, and another time with some old friends,
about the past, about Jeremy. To me, the truth of what
happened was becoming too apparent to ignore. So I
would say the words: "I wasn't there when he died."

And I would think: The doctor said not to go. But I
shouldn't have listened. If only I could tell the story again,
differently.

Charles and the others always tried to comfort me.

"You were so young then," Johnny and Catherine excused my behavior.

"You did the best you could," Charles reminded me gently.

"You can't blame yourself for what happened."

They didn't really understand. I didn't blame myself for what happened. He died. No one could have stopped his dying. But what about what didn't happen? Someone must take the blame for the loneliness of a dying child.

There were times when I thought I would explode. The months wore on, and the anxieties grew and multiplied, stealing my energy, making me less and less present to my children, my husband and my daily life.

But somehow, as always, that life went on. Summer came upon us. Missy and Mark learned to swim and Nicholas learned to run. Like mothers everywhere, I followed my youngest around, rescuing Nicholas from disaster, and rescuing our household treasures from Nicholas.

In late August, when I was just about eight months pregnant, I went to New York to attend a conference at the United Nations. One of the other participants was a nurse who specialized in nursing psychology. Amid stimulating talk of Third World development and the economics of justice, Pat and I found each other.

We connected immediately. She was also struggling to remain involved in global concerns while changing diapers and driving carpools. She had drawn me into conversation as soon as we met, congratulating me for my presence at the conference despite such an advanced state of pregnancy. I found myself revealing a little of my story; I had four children already, but one had died. We discussed his medical problem and she asked questions about my other pregnancies. I was nervous. She was getting close.

During the next free afternoon, we talked again about my son. Thoughts I had left unspoken for years began to pour forth. The baby I was carrying kicked and poked, en-couraging me, urging me to consider something new. An hour passed. Two hours. Finally, I knew I could no longer bury the feelings that were burning a hole in my heart. The long-held secret must be told. It had been long enough.

Trembling, I began my confession.

"He needed me and I wasn't there."

Pat started to interrupt.

"No, let me say this," I pleaded with her, remember-ing all of the others who had ever tried to "comfort" me. "Please let me say this. The one person Jeremy needed was the only person he had known for nine months, and I wasn't there. Other people could try, but he needed his mother to love him and help him die."

My shame was choking me. I had never felt so close to despair.

"He was alone, all alone. While he was dying, I was watching the leaves, and thinking about my pain. I should have held him and kissed him. I should have been there to love him. He needed me."

Pat was holding me, urging me gently to go on.

"I just want him to forgive me."

I let myself sink into long, uncontrolled sobs. Pat waited, her arms still around me.

"Molly," she began carefully, "we know now that neo-natal death is a very traumatic experience for parents, especially for the mother. Doctors are changing their ap-proach, urging parents to be with their babies, even if they are dying. This is very difficult, because those feelings of confusion and pain are powerful. We're just trying to help them through it."

For an instant, I wondered what it would have been like to have known Pat seven years before. But the thought brought back my most private fears . . . surely I would have run from her. I couldn't have survived the knowing.

"I believe," she continued, "what happened to you is that doctors, well-meaning people, and the miracle of drugs kept you from the process of grief. I doubt that you've done it yet. You were never allowed to say goodbye. You never went through the psychological rituals of disbelief, denial, anger, acceptance. You never started to mourn because you were kept from the object of your mourning.

She stopped to watch me. I was totally immersed in her words. "If I were you, Molly, I would be terribly, terribly angry. But besides that, you must take this day, this time, right now to begin your period of mourning."

I was afraid to believe her. I didn't want to blame anyone. I had never blamed the doctors, my family, or even God for what I suspected was my enormous violation of motherhood. I had believed that I should take responsibility for the things I did and didn't do.

Pat's eyes locked into mine. "And Molly, don't be afraid to remember the way it was. You were different then, younger, not nearly as experienced, or as wise, as you are now. That's not an excuse, Molly. That's a fact."

I looked down at my bulging abdomen, caressing it gently. Something seemed to be changing. For so long, I had only pretended to understand. Perhaps there really was an explanation for my behavior that wasn't make-believe.

"I have always needed to acknowledge Jeremy's existence, to claim him as my son," I said, nodding to myself as I spoke. "Maybe that was because I never got to be his mother. I didn't know how it felt to be a mother. Now I do."

I hesitated, but Pat was also nodding her head firmly. With some small surge of confidence, I went on.

"If it happened now, I don't think that I would be so afraid. Perhaps I could somehow find the courage to help my child die. If I could do it all again, I would hold him. He would know how loved he was, even if he was dying."

Pat reacted quickly.

"Jeremy knew you loved him, Molly, but some of the people around you didn't know that. In their desire to shield you from pain, they lost you to it."

We walked around tree-lined New York streets for another hour, talking about the things I could do to continue the process of grief that had begun. A gravestone and funeral might help. I would try not to blame myself. I would try not to ask to be forgiven.

I went home from New York knowing that the remembering had been good for me. What I didn't know was that it was necessary for my very survival. For while I was confronting my past, in no way was I owning it. A chance conversation with my mother began to illuminate this need.

We were talking on the phone. I rarely shared my most intimate thoughts with her, but on this day I needed to talk, and I was grateful that she was there.

I told her about Pat and my experience in New York. As I talked, I began to sense that this conversation might lead to disaster, but I was compelled to go on. I talked about the doctors and the drugs. I confided in her that recently I had been trying to deal with some painful memories. I should never have told her that I wanted to buy a gravestone.

She was quick to respond. "I wanted a gravestone at the time, but you said no, so I thought I shouldn't interfere." From that moment on, the love in her voice was lost to me; where she poured forth her own anguish, all I was able to hear was self-pity. "You say you didn't grieve. Well, I know that I grieved. You don't know how I grieved. I was just so upset. That darling little boy."

She went on, recalling her own sleepless nights and lonely tears. With each word, my anger mounted.

Struggling to sound calm, I spoke deliberately.

"I was just trying to share with you some of my feelings."

Her voice began to falter. Was she the child or was I? "Molly, I just don't want to talk about this anymore. I just can't."

Inside of me, the anger exploded into rage. After a terse goodbye, I slammed down the receiver. The phone toppled off the counter, and I kicked it across the room. Just then Charles walked in.

"How dare she, how dare she!" I shouted for all the neighbors to hear. "How dare she take my pain and make it hers!" I was sure that she had stolen the only tie I had with my son.

"She can't have it. He was my baby, not hers. Can't she even allow me suffering of my very own?"

After a while my husband, who had been listening patiently, took my trembling hands into his. Without a trace of unbelief, he looked into my eyes.

"Your mother loves you, and she loved Jeremy. She, too, has needed to grieve."

I started to object.

"Molly, I do understand your feelings. But just who is it that you are so angry at?"

I didn't know. I didn't want to know. Eventually I understood that I would never confront my mother with those ugly feelings. The baby was due to arrive soon. I was afraid that I would become so angry that I would deny her the pleasure of her new grandchild. Anyway, it would take too much energy, energy I didn't have to give, to confront her, and to confront myself.

I wondered how my unborn child was surviving this emotional roller coaster.

> The real problem isn't hate, no, not hate. But shame, yes, shame.
>
> (Elie Wiesel, *The Gates of the Forest*)

One night, a week before delivery, I had a dream. I had delivered another baby boy. He was sick, just as Jeremy had been. Same condition, same story, same cast of characters . . . except for me. I acted entirely differently. In the dream I never let him go. I cried, I grieved, I felt devastation, but I never let him go. I told him that I loved him, and he died in my arms. Then I woke up.

Lying in bed, I searched for the meaning of that dream. When it came, I could hardly believe it. Could it be that the fear I had been feeling about the health of the new baby might really be desire? Was I daring God to give me another sick child, so that I could prove that I would act differently? It seemed so clear.

I am different, I thought. I am who I am now. Just to be sure, I pleaded with God to send me a healthy child. I didn't want any mix-ups.

Gino James was born on October 10, 1980, healthy and perfect.

The Jeremy-feelings, now so familiar, all but disappeared during the busy activity of Gino's first year. But after his birthday, with what would have been Jeremy's ninth birthday approaching, I began to remember again, and the pain came rushing back, this time with more vengeance than ever before.

Panic. Humiliation, depression, desire that would never be fulfilled. In all the years before, it had never been like this. I couldn't talk about him, I couldn't even mention his name. I hid from the thoughts, terrified of the feelings that would always follow.

November 12, 1981. My vision of hell arrived disguised as Jeremy's birthday. I did not know who I was or who I had been. I lived and died in a single day.

I feel the wound reopening. From the depth of the abyss, the years soar up, unchecked, snatching my heart and pounding it violently against my chest. Anguish grips me, as though I were about to meet something as absolute, as decisive, as pure as the death of a child at dawn.

(Elie Wiesel, *A Beggar in Jerusalem*)

In desperation, I reached out to a loving friend, one who had not heard my story before. I craved reassurance and affirmation.

Even over the phone her voice filled me with hope. I was searching for the magic words that would bring me peace. She was loving, as always, deeply moved by my obvious pain. In a moment of silence, I knew that the words I needed would not come from her. I had been foolish to expect them. The only magic was her great love for me.

"What I do sometimes, when I'm missing someone I've loved, is I talk to them in my prayer. It makes me feel close again."

It was a good idea, I thought, but I was afraid of what Jeremy might say.

During the rest of the day, the nightmare continued. Charles was there again, as he had been many times before. I sensed him struggling to get inside of my pain, trying to make a difference. I had long since stopped expecting him to share my suffering. His grief was his own. At least he had said goodbye.

I awoke on November 13 sick with exhaustion. Alone in our bed, I felt trapped in total futility. The children came in, climbing into the bed with me, asking me questions, beginning their day. I looked at them through empty eyes and wondered if they were real. Suddenly I was aware that I was missing precious moments. What were they saying? Did one of them need me? The nightmare of the day before was a thief, robbing me of that which mattered most. I knew that radical change was needed . . . for their sake, and for mine.

On November 14 I ordered a simple flat marker for Jeremy's grave.

On December 13 I went to see Carl Geraty. He was very open and warm, not at all the way I remembered him. I told my story. His head bowed, he listened quietly. I told him that I felt it might be more helpful to explain to parents their options, and urge them to be with their children. Had he changed his philosophy in recent years?

He looked up. "You're being very kind, Molly. I remember what happened. I kept you from your child, as did your other doctors, the drugs and even your extended family, however loving they thought they were being.

"I would never do that today. We help the parents to be close to their infants, to begin the grief process, to go through each step, to live with dying."

I felt satisfied and relieved. The responsibility really hadn't been all mine. I was thankful for his honesty. Before I left, he reached out and grasped my hands firmly.

"Molly, don't get me wrong. You're a vital, loving human being who is living with a very painful problem. We have to do something about that birthday before next year."

He gave me the name of a psychologist.

> His face grew hard: "You're my friend and I want to know everything."
> I trembled, my breathing quickened, my nostrils flared. He wants to know everything, I thought. He isn't afraid to know everything.
> (Elie Wiesel, *The Town Beyond the Wall*)

One week after Christmas, I walked into the office of Dr. Terry Johnston. I had advised many friends to seek counseling, but when it came to taking my own advice, I felt anxious and self-conscious.

Those feelings evaporated quickly. Terry had ten

children of her own. We shared similar political views, spiritual struggles, and what Terry called "our best guess about parenting." I was enjoying her immensely when she reminded me that it was time to tell my story.

The words poured out easily. While she listened, Terry's face seemed to swallow me up with compassion. When I was done, she smiled broadly.

"Guess what?"

I smiled back, curious.

"My birthday is November 12."

Despite the solemnity of the moment, we laughed together at such a coincidence. A sign. I couldn't hope for much more; I would trust her completely.

"There is something inside of you, Molly, that is keeping you from being whole. You must confront it and own it, so that you can be who you are."

She walked me to the door. She was so confident.

"You can do it. I'll help you. We'll do it together."

And so I began to remember. But this time, it would be different.

> They walked, and the steps echoing more or less together off the sidewalk said: No, you are not alone, but two, two, two.
> (Elie Wiesel, *The Town Beyond the Wall*)

Shortly after my dear friend suggested it, I tried to go to Jeremy in prayer. Afterwards, I even wrote it down, hoping I might never forget. It was a prayer of consolation, but one which only began to touch the source of my pain . . .

The prayer was a meditation in which Jesus came to take me to know God. He had to tug at me because I was reluctant to go and seemed to be stuck in my place. But he kept trying, gathering me up more and more firmly in his arms. Finally I let go, and we went off.

I felt as though we were floating. I buried my head in his shoulder and closed my eyes, allowing myself to be a child again. He leaned down his head to cover me up even more. His arms seemed enormous, loving.

When I finally looked up, I saw a warm light. I knew that the light was God. I could feel love radiating from the light. Then my infant son was brought to me, wrapped up securely in a soft blanket. He began to nuzzle at my breast, and then he nursed eagerly. Gradually he was content, and I watched him drift off to sleep in my arms.

It was as if time had not gone by. My child knew me and I knew him. He didn't seem to care about anything except being with me. Why was that, I asked myself? And then I knew. It was because he was so close to the Creator, to the beginning and end of everything. All he knew was to love wholly and unconditionally. I held him, taken by this moment, yet unaccountably anxious to move on.

. . . The prayer was a gift. Yet even so great a gift was not enough.

Entering the Night

Thank you, my boy. Thank you for disturbing
me, shaking me. Thank you for crossing my path. I
desperately needed you. Thank you for forcing my
hand; you did it in time."

(Elie Wiesel, *The Oath*)

For the moment, the emotional crisis passed. My time
with Terry was a luxury that I deeply appreciated. I didn't
know exactly where all of this was leading, but I was finally
willing to proceed.

Order returned to my life. Indeed, order was a necessity; my days overflowed with the demands of raising four
small children. Beyond the family, I had decided that my
political and social concerns needed a stronger, even formal-
ized spiritual base. Gradually, I had pulled back from some
of my activities and withdrawn from various religious orga-
nizations so that I could pursue a master's degree in theology
at the Graduate Theological Union in Berkeley.

Charles had gone to graduate school earlier in our
marriage, and now was enthusiastic about my endeavor.
But even with his help, the children's enormous needs and
unpredictable daily lives limited me to taking just one class
each quarter.

It didn't matter. In fact, I wanted to go slowly, so as to savor all the things I was learning. Each course I chose seemed to be better than the last. In the beginning, I was especially drawn to courses on scripture, both the Old and New Testaments. But my favorite courses by far were those that mixed religion and politics.

In January of 1982 I fought the long lines of registration to enroll in a class in Liberation Theology that would be taught by Protestant theologian, Robert McAfee Brown. The course engaged us in a new approach to religion and politics, as seen through the eyes of the oppressed. I was fascinated, and thoroughly enlightened. I was also deeply impressed with Bob Brown.

So in April, despite the fact that this was hardly the way to pursue my academic career, I decided to enroll in whatever course Bob would be teaching. "The Theology of Wiesel's Novels" was how it read on the class offering sheet. In the registration line, I found out that the course was about a Jewish man and his writings. It didn't really matter. If Robert McAfee Brown chose him, so would I. And in that way, Elie Wiesel entered my life.

"In the beginning," Bob told us on the first day of class, "the message of Elie Wiesel will not be a comfortable discovery."

It was true. It was a dreadful awakening.

I had returned home from that first day curious enough. After the children were in bed, I picked up our first assignment, the book *Night*, Elie Wiesel's account of the horrifying events of his past. Tired as I was, I couldn't stop reading.

What is it that happened when I met Elie Wiesel? I will try to remember everything.

Bob had begun the story in class that day. Elie was only 14 when he and his family were taken from their hometown of Sighet, in Transylvania, to the Nazi death camp at Auschwitz. On the night he arrived, his mother and little sister, Tzipora, were sent to the right, and Elie and his father went to the left. Elie remembers only an instant of this parting that would be forever. The "right" at Auschwitz meant fire and death.

Then Bob had shared with us excerpts from Elie's writings. I thought that I had understood the Holocaust. But the power of this survivor's words retold the story until I knew I understood nothing. The event is unspeakable, Elie insists, and yet he dares to speak . . . Image upon image, testimony upon testimony, the suggestion of suffering and death too terrible, too inconsolable for the memory of any but the dead themselves. Indeed, it was not only the tale, but the telling.

Despite Bob's careful introduction, I was not prepared for the experience of reading the memories of this storyteller. The power of Elie's remembering invaded my imagination, pulling me deeper into the abyss of sin that destroyed a whole people, a past, present and future, and even a God.

The pages of Elie's *Night* led me, as so many others had been led, into the darkest corner of human history, to recall, and to witness, the consummate evil which thrived there:

> Never shall I forget that night, the first night in camp, which has turned my life into one long night, seven times cursed and seven times sealed. Never shall I forget the smoke. Never shall I forget the little faces of the children, whose bodies I saw turned into wreaths of smoke beneath a silent blue sky.
>
> Never shall I forget those flames which consumed my faith forever.
>
> Never shall I forget that nocturnal silence which deprived me, for all eternity, of the desire to live. Never shall I forget those moments which murdered my God and my soul and turned my dreams to dust. Never shall I forget these things, even if I am condemned to live as long as God himself. Never.
>
> (Elie Wiesel, *Night*)

Scarcely believing, I read these words over and over. Elie's version of reality threatened the limits of what I had thought to be possible. How could this be, I thought to myself, that little children were burned alive on a pile of wood and petrol? Why, why, why, in a world where children ask only to be lifted up into our arms and comforted? The answer, I found, was that the children were burned alive because the gas chambers were full of adults.

Yes, I should have thought of that. The logic of Auschwitz.

I returned to class the next week in a considerably more somber mood. My classmates, too, had been shaken by Wiesel's story. Bob helped us along, taking us back, again and again, through the tragic events.

I found myself mysteriously drawn to this man. I thought of him as Elie, and used his first name when I spoke of him in class. I wanted to know him, to get inside of him. There was a lesson here for me, but it was not yet clear. I wanted to learn how he survived; it was as if my own survival was dependent upon his.

No one, it seemed to me, could continue after the loss of everything and everyone he had ever known and loved. Indeed, for a long time it seemed to Elie that death had triumphed that night. For him, there were ten years of self-imposed silence. But eventually he broke that silence with *Night*, the devastating recollection of the precise events, just as they happened, which marked not only "the death of his childhood" and the murder of his family, but the extermination of six million Jews, a million and a half children. Elie Wiesel had come to understand that survival meant never to forget.

This was his secret: He survived by remembering. His memories stalked him, intent upon the kill, until he turned to face them. The ghosts tormented him, sure of his fear, until he told their story. The curse of remembering was harsh, but there was a blessing, too. This knowing, which finally made holy the evidence of the past, was a transforming grace.

In the days that followed, I read on, searching especially for Elie's memories of the children. I cried; I died a little inside. Anytime he mentioned them, my heart would threaten to break. First, there were the little children being delivered into the pit of fire in *Night*. Then in *Dawn* and *Ani Maamin*, there was the baby who wouldn't stop crying, and the mother whose smothering hand silenced him forever in a futile attempt to save the others. There was Tevye the Tailor's ten children, some who couldn't even stand on their own feet, who lined up from oldest to youngest in front of a firing squad, holding hands to die together in *A Beggar in Jerusalem*. And Mendele, in *The Town Beyond the Wall*, never shall I forget Mendele, who kept the vow of silence through a horribly painful death to try to save the woman who had given him life.

Then it began to happen. When Elie remembered a million and a half children, I remembered my own. The hand of the little boy holding onto Madame Schacter became my Nicholas' hand, trembling as he grows ever more fearful of the fire that will take them, too; the "little faces of the children, whose bodies I saw burned into wreaths of smoke," became the faces of my Melissa and Mark; the baby who had to be silenced became my Gino, just telling me in the only way he knows how that he is afraid.

Frightening, anxious moments of connection followed. His story was so devastating, yet the temptation to remain there with him and the ghosts of the children were too strong to resist. And when I did let go, my soul was deeply disturbed with hideous imaginings. A child, *perhaps my child*, wrenched from my arms, thrown onto the pyre, writhing and screaming. I could hear it, a tiny baby scream in the night. *There was a time and place where this had actually come to pass.*

The gruesome death of a helpless, innocent child . . . the image was almost too much to bear. And then, in my mind, I turned to that mother who watched her first-born disappear into the night. Not a single touch, no lasting embrace, no goodbye. And I knew.

I had entered, in the small way that I could, into Elie's experience. It was as if I was under a spell, seduced by the truthfulness of his memory of total, unspeakable suffering. But there was something else. Once in a while, these memories of Elie's, so vivid, so deeply meaningful, were strangely familiar.

> What is at stake is your life, your survival! Do not forget, do not forget!
>
> (Elie Wiesel, *Souls on Fire*)

In May of 1982 I learned I was to come face to face with Elie Wiesel, whose message had so captivated my mind. Bob, who is a close friend of Elie's, had arranged for members of the class to meet with him after his lecture at the university in a somewhat more intimate setting. I approached this event sure that destiny had somehow arranged things correctly. Of course I must meet him. I must know more.

Charles and I arrived early for the lecture and found seats near Bob Brown and some of my classmates. Bob gave me a warm smile when we came in. Does he sense, I wondered, how much this man has come to mean to me? We waited while the large auditorium filled with people, many of them wearing yarmulkes. Again, I felt strangely close to the storyteller; these were his people, the generation after the six million, and the next generation after them. Elie walked out onto the stage and sat down at a little desk, looking quite like the rebbe, *the teacher*, I decided.

His talk was wonderful, although I was distracted by his voice. It was gentle, yet firm and unafraid; it was sad and mysterious, yet delightful to listen to. Afterwards we walked to a nearby Jewish center for our private time with Elie.

The "private" meeting turned out to be about 40 lucky guests crowded into the center's library. The room itself was a little corner of Elie's world. We wandered around the shelves, stopping to look at a copy of the *Torah*, and I fantasized about Elie's childhood as a student in his hometown of Sighet.

The chairs and couches were quickly filled, and the guests, who included my classmates, the Jewish students from the center, and a few others who had simply heard a rumor about Elie's visit, waited with obvious excitement for the start of the discussion. Bob had asked us to prepare questions for Elie beforehand, so that his friend would not be left without a place to begin. I watched the two of them sitting together on one of the couches, their heads bent in quiet conversation. How nice it would be to be sitting between them, I imagined, but how terrible to intrude on their secret. The magic of their friendship warmed the room and encouraged us to reach out to the visiting storyteller.

As I waited for a chance to ask a question, I wondered how in the world Bob could have ever doubted us. It seemed quite clear that everyone in the room had something to ask of Elie Wiesel.

He listened to each question intently, and answered each one of us in a voice that was so quiet, there was hardly another sound in the room as we strained to hear every word. He seemed very weary, and very sad, as always.

> I hear a voice within me telling me to stop
> mourning the past. I too want to sing of love and of its
> magic. I too want to celebrate the sun, and the dawn
> that heralds the sun.
>
> (Elie Wiesel, *"Why I Write"*)

After about an hour Bob closed off the discussion. The
guests stood around and shared coffee and more informal
conversation, reluctant to leave. I pulled Charles over to
where Bob and Elie were still surrounded by a few linger-
ing students and guests of the center. Finally, it was our
turn. When Bob introduced me to Elie Wiesel, the rebbe
took my hands into his.

Bob told Elie that I was a leader in the local peace
movement. Elie said he was pleased to meet me. I didn't
say anything. Later I reflected that I must have seemed like
a silly school girl meeting the man of her dreams. It was
this man, I thought at the moment of our meeting, who
watched his family die, who heard the cries of the children, who entered the night which has no end.

Elie moved on to meet the others, and Bob whispered
to me, "You touched him — you see, he's real."

Feeling more than a little embarrassed, I wished that
I could tell Bob how I was feeling. Having touched him,
the connection that I couldn't seem to resist had been confirmed. It could continue now. There was still more for me
to learn from Elie Wiesel.

Instead, I laughed and reached out to Bob for a hug.
And I felt sure, somewhere in that warm embrace, that my
teacher knew I loved this rebbe, too.

Only a few days after Elie's talk, I went to visit Jeremy's grave. I knew the marker I had ordered in December
had been set by now. It had been nine years since I had
come to find him; the only other time was about six weeks
after he died. I wandered around the huge cemetery, trying to remember where the children's plots were. After an

hour of going in circles, I saw a row of large markers that looked familiar. Behind it would be the infants and children. I tried to find his row, his place. No marker. Suddenly I knew that he should be here. I got down on my hands and knees, searching for a little stone number 62. What have they done with him? A demon inside of me was doubting his existence. His little body in its wooden coffin, had it dissolved to dust so soon? Had they buried another in his grave? Tears fell in the grass as I frantically searched for the place where my son and his name should be.

Eventually, I had to check the cemetery office to be sure. They were very apologetic. The stone had not been set. They would get right on it.

I went back to Jeremy's grave, and I knew. Six million dead, without graves or names, and Elie held them in his heart as a living graveyard. For him, all that was left of the past was an enormous black cloud.

> Forget the cloud? The black cloud which is Grandmother, her son, my mother. What a stupid time we live in! Everything is upside down. The cemeteries are up above, hanging from the sky, instead of being dug in the moist earth.
>
> (Elie Wiesel, *The Accident*)

I remembered the moment I had considered cremating my son, and I thanked God for the wisdom of a grieving grandmother that kept me from such a decision. In her own way, she had understood: The grief could only end if a place could be found for it to begin. How blessed to have a place where I can find more than ashes, where I can touch his name in the stone and know with all certainty that once he was here with me.

A Child at Dawn

> Memory . . . is both a graveyard and a kingdom.
> It has been a graveyard; now it can begin to be a king-
> dom, opening up a future "whose newness," David
> confides in us, "still makes me dizzy." A blessed state.
> Better than the equilibrium of despair.
>
> (Robert McAfee Brown, *Elie Wiesel, Messenger
> to All Humanity*)

During the last weeks of the course, Elie Wiesel became my constant companion. I talked about him often,
with Charles, with little Melissa, now a sensitive eight-
year-old, and with just about anyone who would listen. He
became more and more present once a week when Terry
and I met, especially when we spoke about the child who,
in spite of all I had remembered, in spite of all I had
learned, was still lost to me.

Immersed in the past, I was working hard to find
something new, something unexpected that would transform the present. Terry urged me on, firmly and lovingly.

"You must do it, Molly," she would say, her face alive
with belief and hope. And so, over and over again, I remembered.

I was surprised at how clear it all was. Images of the
week that Jeremy lived and died unfolded before me, un-

changed by time, secrets thought to be sealed forever, now
being cautiously retold. I studied the mother in the memories and wondered why she had acted the way she did. And
then, dismally, I would remember that the mother was
me.

Could the past be relived so that it came out differently? I looked to my ally, Elie Wiesel, and I knew the answer. The past would not change because of the remembering.

*It will always be so sad that I allowed myself to be sep-
arated from my little boy. It will always be so sad that we
did not say goodbye. Who did this terrible thing? Someone
must take the blame for the loneliness of a dying child.*

Again the guilt, ravaging the heart and stilling all
hopefulness, held me hostage in a story with no ending.
There is more, I thought desperately, there must be more
that can be told. The pain could not be contained; past and
present became one in the darkness. Yet the next step was
elusive.

I became determined: I would search for an ending to
my story.

> "Look at the sky," Pedro said. "It's getting light.
> The night's disappearing."
> (Elie Wiesel, *The Town Beyond the Wall*)

The newness that I was seeking began, not surpris-
ingly, in the words of Elie Wiesel, in the dark places of his
memory, in the night which contains the truth. I remember. I was, for some reason, alone in our house. Curled up
in a chair in our living room, I was reading another of
Elie's stories, feeling familiar feelings of connection.

As the divine plan of all storytellers would have it, it
was in Elie's memory of another mother and another son,
who lived long ago, that I saw myself most clearly. It was

in the other's story, and what happened to me when I felt her pain and shared her guilt, that I began to find the transforming grace. It was Elie and his ghosts who were to be my sweet liberators.

Elie called them out, this mother and her son, gently and lovingly. He didn't reveal much about them; when we read Elie Wiesel, we know the setting: the camps, the selection, the screams of separation, the abrupt ending of all hope. As for me, his words were sufficient. And I knew that the agony I felt when I read the story of this mother was never mine alone:

> "I should have rushed forward, gone with him. He was so small, so far away."
>
> "Try not to think about it anymore," said my Father.
>
> "I can't."
>
> "Make the effort; you must. You can't go on like this. You have no right to. What you did, others have done. By accusing yourself, you condemn all the mothers who did what you did. You are unfair to them."
>
> Her head was tossing on the pillow. "No, no," she said. "I did not behave well. I should have understood. And refused to be separated from my little boy."
>
> Though awake, she was still following her ghost and her breath was halting.
>
> (Elie Wiesel, *The Oath*)

Yes, that is it. Who would have thought that anyone else could have known?

I sat shivering in my chair, suddenly aware of the stillness of the house.

Yes, I know how you must have felt. It will never be over. Death happens, intruding into our ordered delusion of forever and ever. Death is the story with a beginning and no end.

It must be the same with me. My chance has come and gone. We did not say goodbye. He lay dying in his little bed alone. Once in a while, a stranger wearing a mask over her mouth rocked him in a wooden rocking chair. I did not behave well. I should have understood, and refused to be separated from my little boy.

My little boy. It is so hard to let go. If only we could be together for one more moment. Could the wound still be healed, and the sin still forgiven?

But once, another mother in another time and place had tried, and failed:

> He comes, looks at me and goes away. I run after him, but the distance between us does not diminish. And so I shout, I scream. He stops and so do I . . . I begin to shout again, to scream, but he has already disappeared. He is angry with me, I know that he is angry with me. I shouted too late.
>
> (Elie Wiesel, *The Oath*)

These haunting words of the storyteller found a fine home in my wounded spirit. Two voices from deep within me pierced the silence, arguing relentlessly.

It is too late, one would say.

To which the other would reply, *I cannot give you up. Not yet.*

I slammed the book shut in order to silence all the voices. It was my turn to speak:

Yes, Elie, you have done well.

My fears and weaknesses leap out at me from the pages of your past and the stories of your beloved six million. But your lesson, rebbe, is not just to confront death in the past, but to confront life in the present. And I can be patient, just as you have been. I must be patient. There is a way out of this hell, and its name is love.

> Every death leaves a scar, and every time a child laughs it starts healing.
>
> (Elie Wiesel, *The Gates of the Forest*)

It was as inevitable as turning to the next page. The mystery of memory, once embraced, gave way to the promise of possibility. The new kingdom, at long last, was opened up.

The book was Elie Wiesel's *A Jew Today*, and the passage was called "A Man and His Little Sister." I had read these moving words several times before. But when on the last day of class my teacher, Elie's good friend, read them aloud to us, they became for me the greatest gift of Elie's memory and imagination. It began:

> Will you remember me? Tell me. Will you remember me, too?
> *Of course.*

It was a conversation, a quiet little talk between two people who loved each other. They lingered over the memories of the past, so as to speak to each other in the present:

> But you will speak even when you do not see me?
> *I shall try.*
>
> You will say that I liked to sing? That I liked to listen to you sing?
> *I shall say that too.*
>
> And that I loved the Holy Days?
> *You radiated joy.*
>
> And Shabbat? You won't forget to say how much I loved Shabbat?
> *It made you glow.*
>
> And the Shabbat songs?
> *You sang them at the table.*
>
> And you will speak of my love of God?
> *Yes, little sister.*

And my grief at losing you, losing all of you, you
will speak of that too?
I shall carry it inside me.

And finally, they brought forth the memory of a terrible, terrible hurt. Quickly, recognition resounded in my
being; instantly I knew those feelings of separation, regret,
grief.

One more thing.
Yes?

When you speak of your little sister leaving you
like that, without a hug, without a goodbye, without
wishing you a good journey, will you say that it was
not her fault?
It was not your fault.
(Elie Wiesel, *A Jew Today*)

There we were, Jeremy and I, living inside Elie's
memory of his little sister, Tzipora. Was Jeremy Tzipora,
or was I? I wanted so much to understand, and to hold on
to what I recognized in Elie's words. The parting between
Elie and his little sister had taken only an instant. It was
barely recognizable as the important moment that it was,
and later he struggled to recapture it and re-create more of
the image than his mind had recorded. The anguish that
must have caused him! I, too, suffered for the memory of
an instant, and I, too, was searching for the one person
who could offer a healing word, and a new ending.

Again and again, over the days that followed, I
looked back at this scene. I wanted to clap and shout, and
celebrate their victory over death. *You did it! You refused
to be separated!* And I think now that my heart knew how
close I was to the miracle.

Suddenly, it sounded like a simple task. Jeremy and I
must talk.

I envisioned such a moment, and planned for the joy

it could bring. A soothing, completing moment, when I would be forever distracted from searching for what couldn't be found, when a new light would penetrate the darkness and change forever my relationship with that one unique pain.

For months, I hoped it would happen. Yet every time I tried, I stopped short of listening for a reply. I prayed for patience, I trembled when I looked for him. And then one day it happened, because Jeremy was the one who began.

Dialogue Between a Son and His Mother

Were you happy when I was born?
Oh yes. Dad and I were both very happy. We even cried for joy.

I knew you were happy. I just wanted you to tell me. I remember how they put me on your stomach. They didn't leave me there long enough, though.
I didn't think it was long enough, either. It was my first time, and I didn't know I could make my own decisions.

So you remember my first cry?
Yes.

And the first time they brought me to you?
Yes. You were beautiful. You had smooth olive skin and brown hair. You had long fingers like mine.

Everyone said I looked like Dad. And that was nice. But you know what?
What?

I wanted to look like you.
You did? Why?

91

Because you had carried me with you for so long. You were everything to me. I wanted to be just like you.
I hadn't thought of that.

What else do you remember, Mother?
Lots of things. I remember the way your eyes opened and closed and the way your hands moved in your sleep.

What else?
I remember the way you breathed and the way you cried.

What else?
I remember your little foot sticking out of the blanket. It was so cute.

And when they undressed me for you?
I was afraid you might be cold.

I was. I was so glad to be in your arms. It felt safe and warm.
You didn't want to eat.

I'm sorry you were so worried. I could see you frowning, even behind that mask.
I hated that mask.

I know, but it didn't matter. I just wanted to be with you.
I couldn't kiss you through the mask. I don't know why.

You kissed me with your eyes, Mother. I could feel your eyes loving me, especially the night I took the formula. I could feel your eyes following me down the hallway.
That was the last time.

Last time for what?
The last time I held you. Did you miss me after that?

Yes. But then I would just remember you.
Remember me?

Yes. I remembered how warm your body felt. You protected me for nine months. You gave me life. Then you held me for two days. We could look at each other.
Yes, we looked at each other.

You remember? I would close my eyes and imagine you, imagining me.
I have imagined you often.

I remember your heart beating. And you would say my name.
I love that name.

I remember your blond hair and your green eyes. I remember your smile. I remember your tears. I knew you loved me.
But I went away.

Yes, but I could always remember.
I'm sorry. I never said goodbye.

Neither did I. I'm sorry too. We didn't know.
No, we didn't.

Will you tell them about me?
Who?

My sisters and brothers.
Of course.

What will you tell them about me?
Everything.

Will you tell them I didn't cry very much?
Yes.

And that I tried to eat for you?
Yes.

And that you will never forget me?

Neither will they. I will give them my memory of you.

Listen, Mother, I know what we'll do.
What's that?

You tell all those who come after me, and I'll tell all those who came before me.
What will we tell them?

How we loved each other.
I love you, Jeremy.

I love you, Mother.

Epilogue

The Message

Suffering confers neither privileges nor rights; it all depends on how one uses it . . . Neither ends nor means, it can bring him closer to his truth and his humanity.

(Elie Wiesel, *A Jew Today*)

Jeremy and I are different now.

Our suffering, remembered and transformed, is neither over nor continuing. But there remains for us a message — a reminder, a gift. Now I must not only remember, but create anew. What remains for me is to seek the truth and the humanity of that single, devastating embrace we once shared.

I could stop now with my story. But if I did, I would betray this message, and therefore the messenger. We bring the trust of our childhood to the wisdom of our maturity and find how wonderful it can be to be awakened — and changed — by another human being. "Blessed is the one," says Elie Wiesel, "who is capable of surprising and being surprised."

From this messenger, the rebbe, I learned a song of liberation: Do not forget, do not forget. He helped me find the one I had lost, my child whose memory I had buried

before I buried him. But that discovery led me even farther. It released my single memory in the midst of a million
others and I found myself in a new universe of understanding and connection.

The past became my ally. For Elie Wiesel, the past
became his ally in the vision of the ghosts of the six million,
coming to life at Jerusalem's wall, rising up in his defense.
Today, for me, those same ghosts, and a little boy with
brown hair and olive skin, rise up to insist upon the memory and connectedness of all human suffering. The connection was made not in the death of Jeremy itself, but in the
feelings — the loss, the guilt, the endless grief —
experienced in the death of a child.

Some time ago, before I met Elie Wiesel, before
Jeremy and I talked, I found the substance of my daily life
changing. Where once I would be comfortable for days on
end, I was coming to realize that contentment belonged to
some other time and place. Please do not misunderstand. I
could still laugh and sing. I could still make love and enjoy
my daughters and sons. But from within the safe bounda-
ries of life's goodness, I was drawn to contemplation of
deadly evil subduing the joyful, of suffering silencing the
singing, of violence smothering love.

Then, the unexpected. In the midst of this awakening
and in the midst of my hesitant remembering, I met another who had been left behind in the night, one who had
memorized and multiplied my sorrow. This miracle of our
meeting was not the light that shone after years of darkness, but the darkness itself, the night where that which we
fear the most comes to be known.

I entered that night, that frightening place where the
truth of all that has happened is finally, boldly, told. Sur-
prisingly enough, it was only there that at long last we
could say goodbye — Elie and Tzipora, Jeremy and I.

Other voices in that darkness were familiar, but now, because I had traveled there with Elie and Jeremy, they were voices I could better understand.

Alongside my son's tiny goodbye, I heard the goodbyes of so many others. The six million whose anguished cries echo into the present; the daily goodbyes of other mothers as they bury their own tiny victims of poverty and war, greed and indifference — now an agonizing groan that I not only heard, but recognized. For although the experience of suffering has infinite variations, in the darkness the voices that cry out at the final moment of separation are indistinguishable. I had grown from a concerned observer to a more compassionate, empowered companion.

> Open your eyes, don't say a word. Stay where you are, as you are, huddled in the dark. Don't run after images; you must make them yours without running, without calling.
>
> (Elie Wiesel, *The Oath*)

Night. Welcome this unexpected blessing, like the creature that emerges so innocently from the darkness of the mother's womb, the truth which promises a new human possibility.

It seems that the night is ours. In the darkest places of our collective memory, we find what is best left forgotten — our own pain and the pain of others, evil and our own complicity. Yet if our truth and our humanity also lie waiting in those shadows, what else is there for us to do but dismiss our childish confidence in the easy truths of the light of day?

> Whoever walks in the night, moves against night.
>
> (Elie Wiesel, *The Oath*)

And the message?

We must enter the night and remain there. If evil is to be known, and resisted, we must find its home, remember its crimes, unearth its victims. And with every ounce of our humanity, we must connect with those who suffer. For the way of resistance is the way of connection — a daring, stubborn insistence upon remaining human in the face of evil, and of finding one another, despite separation. To see in the dark, to remember, and then to connect.

To be merely bothered by the pain of the world is to sink into the worst of sins (so says the rebbe) — indifference. Faced with the choice between silence and shouting, the only human choice is shouting. One must act, tell what one knows, in order to avoid indifference. One must have courage and, God knows, creativity, in order to resist evil.

The storyteller in me has instructed the resister. Because my pain begins to resemble that which is felt by so many others, and because my suffering escapes my singular experience and joins a whole universe of suffering and sorrow, then to my great surprise, the power of compassion is again confirmed. Despite my hesitation, I claim some small role in the story — yet to be told — of humanity's survival.

November 12, 1982.

The ghosts did not return this year. This time there was no struggle to hide from memory and imagination. The child had been there to greet me at dawn and I had welcomed him, but the image quickly faded. Instead, it would be a day like most other days, full of the disorder and delight brought by the children, and the discomfort brought by the headlines.

During the afternoon I had been to a local Catholic university, part of a panel of people discussing nuclear disarmament. I had been particularly moved by a Jewish woman, a child psychologist, who reminded us again of the deadly consequences of living each of our days under the threat of nuclear annihilation. And I had been deeply disturbed by the accusations of another woman in the audience, a Guatemalan refugee, who said that our visions of peace were naive and typically North American, and neglected the desperate need for economic justice among Third World peoples. By the time I arrived home that evening, I was ready for small talk about small problems. I was greeted at the door by my seven-year-old son.

Mark Joseph has always seemed to know what is important to me. Tonight, he had something he couldn't wait to tell.

"Mom, I saw him, he was right there!"

"Who was there, Mark?" He led me into the room where he quickly pointed to the television screen.

"Our friend, Elie Wiesel." I smiled at Mark's cozy notion of our relationship with the storyteller. What a day for Mark and Elie to find one another.

"What does Elie Wiesel do?" Mark wanted to know.

"He tells stories." I knew what was coming next. Mark's questions are numerous, mostly delightful, and sometimes predictable.

"What kinds of stories?"

"Stories about his childhood, and about the terrible suffering of his people." Mark didn't have another question yet, so I kept going. "Stories about the past, the present, and the future. About hatred, and about love."

"Tell me one about love."

I looked at my son. In Elie's stories, I remembered, love is almost always hidden behind the suffering and the pain. Love is the conclusion we come to when we decide to remain human in the face of evil.

I hadn't even taken off my coat. I could hear sounds

coming from other parts of the house that probably needed my investigation. But my son's eagerness to be with me, to know more, especially on this day, was irresistible.

Pedro, I thought, I should tell Mark about Pedro. Pedro is one of my favorite of Elie's memories. Pedro loved his friend Michael, and he helped the young man to be a survivor, despite the haunting memories of the death camp and the hideous evil of his past. Then Pedro urged Michael to go even further, to begin to defeat evil by reaching out to still another human being. The story of Pedro and Michael is the turning point, for Elie and for all of us. We defy death by doing what is least expected: remaining human, daring to love.

How could I tell Mark about Pedro? There was so much to tell.

While I was deciding, Mark pulled me down to a pile of pillows on the floor and, snuggling in next to me, waited expectantly. Finally, he helped me out.

"Tell me one about when he was a little boy."

Immediately I thought of Szerencsevaros. Elie talks about this small town when he tells the story of Pedro and Michael. Szerencsevaros was the home of Michael's childhood and, I suspect, of Elie's. His home and his childhood, of course, were destroyed, engulfed by the night.

I began, "Did I ever tell you about Szerencsevaros?" As best as I could, I was trying to become the storyteller.

Mark laughed at my beginning. "No, Mom, what kind of name is that?"

"It was a little city. A little city, happy and poor. They used to say, 'even the rich are poor there, and even the poor were happy!'

"The Sabbath was the favorite day of the people of Szerencsevaros. Everyone worked hard all week, so that the Sabbath could be celebrated and enjoyed with enough bread and wine for everyone.

"On Friday evening, when the Sabbath arrived, all of the merchants closed up their shops and hurried home to their families, who were getting ready to go to the synagogue for prayers. And while this was going on, the little city got very, very, quiet.

"Then, if you listened closely, you could begin to hear a song being sung, up and down the streets."

Mark interrupted. "How did it go?"

"I wish I could sing it, Mark. I don't know the tune. But I remember the words:

> "Peace upon you, O Angels of Peace; peace upon you as you come and peace upon you as you go."

Mark couldn't keep still. "I know why you like that song, Mom. It's about peace."

I hugged him. How wonderful to get a glimpse of myself in the eyes of my little boy! I continued, as Elie's story came back to me.

"That song, Mark Joseph, was the welcoming song for the most important people in the city. On Friday night in Szerencsevaros, no one could go hungry, or be lonely. If anyone was alone, or a stranger, he was invited in by one of the families, and then they broke bread together and no one was alone anymore.

"The children had a special job. They watched for a stranger to invite in, because a family without a poor guest at their table would feel guilty, not to be sharing. And even while the people prayed in the synagogue, the poor and the beggars waited. When the prayers were over, the people of the city rushed around, hoping to find a beggar or a stranger to bring home. So before long, everyone of them had been taken."

My son was smiling, his eyes wide open and attentive.

"You see, Mark, in Szerencsevaros, the poor considered themselves to be important. And since they were important, the rich didn't have to feel so guilty about their good fortune. That's why the poor were called 'the angels of peace on the Sabbath.'"

Mark seemed content. After a while, he jumped up and pronounced the story ended:

"That city was upside down, wasn't it!"

I wished Elie had been there.

Mark and the other children had gone to bed. Charles had fallen asleep in our room, waiting for me to end this day. I retreated to the pillows on the floor, thinking about Mark's logic.

A world turned upside down. I considered this possibility. Will it be my children who finally see that growing up means striving to make the dream of Friday night in Szerencsevaros come true? All that is left of this village is its place in Elie's memory, and yet it points the way toward the startling possibility of our salvation. *Remember the past so as to be more alive in the present.* And on this day of days, I knew how true this was. I couldn't imagine what would have happened if I hadn't remembered, if I had continued to avoid the darkness. Remembering made a space for Jeremy and me, re-created our moment, made holy our connection. But there is more. "Re-create the universe," Pedro tells Michael. Remember, and mourn, the child who was burned alive at Auschwitz. Imagine, and celebrate, the child who loved a beggar in Szerencsevaros. And re-create the future. Do we dare hope for such a surprise?

It would seem so. The erection of a moral world on top of the ruins of yesterday can no longer be a pipe dream when the survival of humanity is at stake. The present universe finds evil alive and well, nurtured by our inhumanity, taking form in poverty and power, in racism and war among peoples, and anticipating its final glorious victory in the next Holocaust, that of nuclear destruction.

And yet, the logic of Szerencsevaros defied the logic of Auschwitz, and today defies any logic on earth. Where is it that we begin the great task of re-creation?

Darkness deepened in the room where Mark and I had imagined a place where just people lived together in peace. As I had so many times before, I began to contemplate and organize the risky, arrogant dream of resisting the evils of today's world. But tonight other images would first press into my mind, and the undeniable reality of human suffering, continuing and intensifying at that very moment, dismissed the intellect and scorned understanding.

Who has come here to be with me tonight? Is it my son, or is it another mother's child? How many of them are arriving to bring the shadows to life, to tell the secrets of the darkness? They are filling my arms. I can hardly breathe in their embrace.

Lying there on my pillows, I remembered again the whispered truths that emerge from the night. It would seem that the message of those who suffer to the rest of us is urgency, the urgency of the task of re-creation.

Remember the past, transform the present, re-create the future. It is a race through time in which all of us must take part, hoping we arrive at the future before the Angel of Death.

> The Exterminating Angel has not yet entered the walls and I wonder to whom and to what we are beholden for it. Is it only a postponement? For the moment we are all survivors.
>
> (Elie Wiesel, *The Oath*)

If it is true that for the moment we are all survivors, can we even begin to accept the responsibility? The survivor tells the tale of the past through the eyes of one who was there, without trying to change it or make it understand-able. *Of evil, she must speak of never allowing it to be un-derstood.* The survivor sees the present through the eyes of truth, without trying to excuse it, without trying to pre-tend it is out of reach. *Of despair, she must speak of reject-ing it as a solution.* The survivor warns of the future through the eyes of the prophet, without allowing it to un-fold without us, without denying the danger. *Of the fu-ture, she must speak of history in danger of repeating itself.*

In the room where I remained, I knew there was more than silence and darkness.

What are they waiting for? For me?

> "The only valuable protest, or attitude, is one rooted in the uncertain soil of humanity. Remaining human — in spite of all temptations and humilia-tions — is the only way to hold your own against the other, whatever it may be."
> (Pedro to Michael, in Elie Wiesel, *The Town Beyond the Wall*)

In our uneasy passage from the paralysis of the specta-tor to the activity of the protester, the step that plans for re-creation is to remain human. To reach out to the other . . . to engage in the madness of love.

There is a moment of grace when this happens. It is the moment in which the power of compassion, a power that has been inside of us all along, can no longer be con-tained. The human connection is just too strong. The re-flection is too clear, the suffering too familiar.

I rolled over on the floor to face the bookcase against the wall. My eyes had grown accustomed to the lack of light, and I searched the shelves for one of Elie's books. What is it that he teaches about that moment of grace, when the looking, the aching, gives way to madness? In a world where, as Elie decided, insanity parades around as reason and understanding is disguised as madness, perhaps this is the moment we must consider, and cherish.

I found what I was looking for. And once again, the wisdom of Elie Wiesel captured my imagination and led the way into the darkness, in search of truth. Knowing that I was intruding upon the crowded silence of that night, I read aloud his story about this interval in time, this blessed state, when evil is resisted, humanity spared, and re-creation begun:

> A field.
> Jewish mothers,
> Naked,
> Lead their naked children
> To their sacrifice.
> I see the priests,
> Dressed in black,
> Behind the machine guns,
> And at the peepholes
> Of special installations
> In Birkenau and Treblinka.
> But the mothers
> See nothing.
> I see them,
> These mothers
> And their little girls.
> Gaunt, distraught mothers;
> Tired, frightened children.
> Clumsily, to no avail,
> Some women try to hide
> Their nakedness.
> And I am looking.
> Aching.
> Going mad.
> I snatch a little girl,
> Blue eyes, black hair,
> I snatch her from her mother
> And I run.
> I run as far as my legs will carry me,
> Like the wind,
> Farther than the wind.
> I run,

And while I run,
I am thinking:
This is insane,
This Jewish child
Will not be spared.
I run and run
And cry.
And while I am crying,
While I am running,
I perceive a whisper:
I believe,
Says the little girl,
Weakly,
I believe in you.

(Elie Wiesel, *Ani Maamin*)

I am left in the darkness with only one child in my arms. I am here, looking, aching. The connection happens, the feelings stir, they mount, they soar. Those children are my chldren, those arms my arms, and I can no longer help myself. I, too, have chosen madness.

As happens only once in a while, I prayed an honest, desperate prayer of hope. This was, for me, a precious instant of understanding, understanding both old and new, and I wanted to cling to it, and to feel its power. I believed that a million messengers had already shouted the message of this moment, and now, even to me, one ancient cry of connection returned to help me never to forget.

In Ramah is heard the sound of moaning,
    of bitter weeping!
Rachel mourns her children,
    she refuses to be consoled
    because her children are no more.

(Jeremiah 31:15)

The power of our grief for our children! There is no consolation great enough to end the mourning. Nor should there be. We who can even begin to feel her suffering must never be silent until all suffering has ceased. It is from within our arms that a new power is unleashed, something enormous and untapped, maybe uncontrollable. It is the power of God held in the heart of a mother, put there for safekeeping. It is obsessive, ferocious, unconditional. It is the unbreakable bond between parent and child that is one tiny thread in the infinite bonding between Creator and creation. And once unleashed, this great power, as the rebbe has said, is "mystical madness," the madness of love.

It is mad to love in a world that spins on an axis fueled by threats of mutually assured destruction, by ideological differences which grow into hatred of a nation's people, or a people's race. It is mad to forgive each other, and heal each other, in a world that finds its sick power in the brokenness of its people. When we resort to love, surely we are doing what is least expected.

And hope, when reality tempts us only with despair, must be the least expected act of all.

Eventually, my companions for that night, the little girl, Elie and the survivors, my brown-haired, olive-skinned baby boy retreated into the universe of memory. The darkness which had revealed so much was only an empty room once more. I started for bed, stopping to peer into each room where our children were sleeping.

Nicholas, who always notices yet never trusts the night shadows, had climbed into bed with Gino. They were curled up together perfectly, as if only one brother lay sleeping there. While I was watching them, Nicholas suddenly stretched and turned over in his sleep, and Gino obliged with the same movement, uttering a little giggle in some faraway dream of brothers at play.

I have noticed how my children are always doing what is least expected. Is that a sign of hope? Perhaps they are going mad, too.

In the next room, the clock on Mark's bedside table read one a.m. *Your day is over, Jeremy John.* I brushed back Mark's hair from his face, remembering one son while blessing another.

And finally, Melissa's room, where in the corner in her crib our two-month-old daughter, Kristen Elizabeth, was making the familiar noises of a baby's sleep. I leaned over to kiss her, and then Melissa, who stirred at my touch.

"Hi, Mom," she whispered, trying to wake up.

"Hello. Go back to sleep."

"Mom, I've been wanting to talk to you about something."

Not tonight, I thought, I have been emptied out, and filled up. I have nothing left for you except a goodnight kiss. But she sat up, fully awake, ready for me to listen.

"It's about gymnastics."

Gymnastics. It occurred to me that motherhood meant abandoning one's dreams on very short notice.

Melissa had been preparing for an upcoming competition and I, in a burst of parental enthusiasm, had been pressuring her to do well.

"I'm afraid sometimes," she began with a few tears, "that if I don't win you won't love me as much."

As swiftly as she challenged me, disgrace descended, tempting me to avoid this conversation. But it was too late. The shame that she called forth in me would not be denied. Suddenly I, too, was wide awake.

How could I send her that message, I scolded myself, when on other days I preached the shortcomings of a competitive lifestyle and the necessity of fostering a good self-image in every human being? I hastened to make amends.

"Melissa, I'm so sorry. I have been pressuring you. Please forgive me."

Silence as she thought about forgiving me.

"I will always love you, no matter what. You and the other children are the most important things in my world."

I looked for the words that would speak to her of a love that had no limits.

"I would never give you up."

And then my nine-year-old daughter, who, apparently, had grown up when I wasn't looking, responded without a moment's hesitation:

"Would you give me up for a peaceful world?"

I was shocked. I repeated her question in my head, just to make sure she had really asked it. Finally, I turned to her.

The look on her face was not fear, or sadness, as I might have expected. Instead, when I gazed into those beautiful eyes, I saw determination, understanding and hope, yes, hope.

Slowly, I gave her my answer, watching her closely as I spoke.

"No, Melissa, I wouldn't give you up for anything."

She was glad that I loved her that unconditionally. She expected as much. But at that instant we understood something together, she and I, that neither of us had known quite as well before. We had engaged in the madness of love, and found hope in the other.

> There is more of eternity in the instant which
> unites two people than in the memory of God.
>
> (Elie Wiesel, *The Accident*)

Cuddled close to Charles in our bed, I savored our daughter's courageous words. Her question acknowledged — and blessed — my own questioning, and my commitment, humble as it is, to challenge the human structures which perpetuate suffering and keep us from the peace which God, too, awaits. She had taken my vision

into herself and become hopeful that someday the dream
would become reality. While I was affirming the value of
her one, solitary life, she had run ahead to glimpse the
power of our common humanity. She, too, was beginning
to take on the defiant role of human person, compassionate, connecting, loving, in a world which is flirting with
the extinction of all humanness, of all humanity.

*"I think the whole world has gone Jewish," the Rebbe
shouted, thoroughly bewildered, at no one in particular.
Nevertheless, many people heard him.*

Yes, Elie, this is probably true. Where once a tyrant
plotted to exterminate the entire Jewish race, today the
tyranny of power and greed plots to erase our history, de-
vour our hope, and exterminate the entire human race. Are
we able to rescue those who suffer from this fatalistic
chain? Will anyone mourn the death of a child at dawn,
and dare to breathe the possibility of new life? Yes. The answer is to be found in the human connection, the journey
from separation to solidarity. And in the frantic dance of
the survivors, twirling about in the madness of love, cer-
tain once again that there is still time to defy death and to
speak of continuation.

Yes, my son, it is true. The circle of connection con-
tinues, expanding, becoming stronger. It is in the remembering that we become wise; it is in the wisdom that we
reach out for the other. And it is in the embrace that we
find hope without limitation.

What is there left for us to do?
(Elie Wiesel, *The Gates of the Forest*)

"Charles, are you awake?"

"Yes."

I was so filled with wisdom to be shared that I didn't know where to begin. So I was silent.

He rolled over until I knew he was facing me in the darkness. I could feel his breath on my face.

"How was it today, Mol?"

My husband's question surprised me a little, and moved me.

"It was a good day, Charles. I felt our son here with me, especially tonight, reminding me, teaching me things. Do you know what I mean?"

"I think so." He reached over and found my hand. "Have I told you lately," he continued, "that I believe what you believe? And that I'm glad you're sharing it all with our children?"

He stopped, and I wondered if he was going to say anything else. He breathed a long sigh and I guessed he was drifting back into sleep. But then, I heard his voice again, filling up the silence, at once jubilant and harmonious, as though a choir of six million angels was concluding this midnight gift to me.

"You're a good mother."

I remained very still. Goodnight Charles. Goodnight Jeremy, Melissa. Thank you for proclaiming your belief in me. Thank you for urging me on.

What is there left for us to do? Sleep. Sleep now, for at dawn we must choose madness again, and continue the holy task of re-creation.

Bibliography

The following books by Elie Wiesel have been quoted in the text. The original titles in French and publication dates are in parentheses.

A Beggar in Jerusalem (*Le Mendiant de Jerusalem*, 1968), New York: Random House. 1970.

The Accident (*Le Jour*, 1961), New York: Bantam Books. 1982.

A Jew Today (*Un Juif Aujourd'hui*, 1978), New York: Vintage Books. 1979.

Ani Maamin, A Song Lost and Found Again, New York: Random House, bilingual edition. 1974.

The Gates of the Forest (*Les Portes de la Foret*, 1964), New York: Holt, Rinehart and Winston. 1966.

Night (*La Nuit*, 1958), New York: Bantam Books. 1982.

The Oath (*Le Serment de Kolvillag*, 1973), New York: Avon Books. 1973.

Souls on Fire (*Celebration Hassidique*, 1972), New York: Vintage Books. 1972.

The Town Beyond the Wall (*La Ville de la Chance,* 1962), New York: Holt, Rinehart and Winston. 1964.

"Why I Write." In *Confronting the Holocaust: The Impact of Elie Wiesel.* Edited by Alvin H. Rosenfeld and Irving Greenberg. Bloomington: Indiana University Press. 1978.

Other author and title quoted:

Robert McAfee Brown. *Elie Wiesel, Messenger to All Humanity,* Notre Dame, Indiana: University of Notre Dame Press. 1983.